In *Fingerprint of God: The Church as a Living Body*, Dr. Ron Bryce approaches the biblical concept of the church as a living body through the lens of a medical doctor. He draws insightful conclusions about how believers should function as an organized community and in relationship to the world.

—Scott Wilson
Pastor, Oaks Church; Author, *Clear the Stage*

The most common metaphor used in the New Testament is the physical body. Through Dr. Bryce's medical understanding of anatomy and physiology, with great insight he explores this body metaphor in a thought-provoking way as it is applied to the church, the body of Christ. The book is well written and offers a unique opportunity to rethink the function and ministry of the church. I was stirred to rethink and evaluate the way the local church body relates to one another and ministers effectively in this world. The book brings opportunities for correction and hope to the twenty-first century church.

—Pastor Bruce Zimmerman, ThM,
Waxahachie Bible Church

Dr. Ron Bryce may be the most extraordinary man in principle and purpose that I have ever met. His wisdom is quiet yet piercing; his heart is compassionate, and his faith is dynamic. In his new book, *The Fingerprint of God*, you will be introduced to a new view of the church that comes straight from a physician's perspective. However, this book is not just for scientists or those in the medical profession. It is for all of us who profess a love for Jesus Christ and for His body. You will read it and weep . . . You will read it and be changed . . . You will read it and be healed.

—Carol McLeod
Best-selling author of nine books; Radio host and Bible teacher; Author,
Guide Your Mind, Guard Your Heart, Grace Your Tongue

With humility that comes from life and wisdom that comes from learning, Dr. Ron Bryce writes about a reality that he knows well and loves deeply. As a physician, he sees great meaning in the biblical vocabulary that speaks of the church as "the body of Christ." This means the church is far more than an organization; it is an organism! Reading this book will confirm your worst fears about the sad state of the institutional church today, but far more importantly, it will give you a biblical vision for what is possible when God's redeemed people function as the living body He intends them to be. Filled with personal stories and biblical truth as well as medical science, this book will renew your love for the true church and make you want to be a member. I recommend it!

—STAN KEY
President, the Francis Asbury Society; Former Spiritual Dean
of the Pan-African Academy of Christian Surgeons (PAACS)

Dr. Bryce borrows from his medical training and clinical experience to help us understand that "the body of Christ" is not simply a metaphor. We are to be a living, active, divine organism reflecting the transformation possible through Jesus Christ and the vitality of the kingdom. And as our physical bodies leave fingerprints as evidence of their presence, we should leave fingerprints on this world. *Fingerprint of God* inspires us to be an effective body of Christ.

—GENE RUDD, MD
Senior Vice President, Christian Medical & Dental Associations

FINGERPRINT

OF

GOD

THE CHURCH
AS A LIVING BODY

FINGERPRINT

OF

GOD

RON BRYCE, MD

BROWN
CHRISTIAN
PRESS
A DIVISION OF
BROWN BOOKS PUBLISHING

Fingerprint of God
The Church as a Living Body

Brown Christian Press
16250 Knoll Trail Drive, Suite 205
Dallas, Texas 75248
www.BrownChristianPress.com
(972) 381-0009

Names: Bryce, Ron.
Title: Fingerprint of God : the Church as a Living Body / Ron Bryce, MD.
Description: Dallas, Texas : Brown Christian Press, a division of Brown Books
    Publishing, [2018] | Includes bibliographical references.
Identifiers: ISBN 9781612542690
Subjects: LCSH: Jesus Christ--Mystical body. | Church. | Religion and science.
Classification: LCC BV600.5 .B79 2018 | DDC 262/.77--dc23
A New Era in Publishing®

ISBN 978-1-61254-269-0
LCCN 2018937713

Printed in the United States
10 9 8 7 6 5 4 3 2 1

For more information or to contact the author, please go to
www.FingerprintofGodBook.com.

This book is dedicated to all members of the Church currently under attack around the world. To Christians unable to practice their faith in freedom without fear of covert or overt persecution, incarceration, or execution: we feel your pain. We grieve and bleed with you. We are one in the body of Christ.

CONTENTS

ACKNOWLEDGMENTS

I am greatly indebted to the countless people who allowed me the privilege of caring for them as a physician.

I would like to recognize the nurses, physicians, and other professionals in the healing arts who give their time, energy, and resources for the betterment of mankind. It has been my privilege to have worked with some of the most giving, tireless, and selfless people imaginable. I am proud to be considered one of their peers.

I am also thankful for the pastors and church leaders who are called upon to give of themselves during this life so that the body of Christ may continue to live and flourish. Their prayers and tears for those under their care are the lifeblood of the body. If not for ministers heeding the call of God on their lives, the body of Christ could not become actualized in this world.

My thanks to Ken Walker, who encouraged me to expand my original musings to a full-length manuscript, added relevant research material, and pulled personal anecdotes from the depths of my memory.

And special thanks to Hallie Raymond for her thoughtful changes to my manuscript, and the rest of the team at Brown Books Publishing Group for all of their hard work in making this book a reality.

I am especially thankful for my wife, Lydia. I love her with all my heart. She is a constant help and encouragement.

Most of all, I am thankful for Jesus Christ, the Giver of all life.

—Ron Bryce, MD
Dallas, Texas
October 2018

INTRODUCTION

LOVE IS THE KEY

*We shall never understand the nature of the human body if we
begin thinking about the single members severed from the body
and try to conceive of the body as a mere sum of hundreds of those
members. We shall never understand Paul's concept of the church
if we begin our theological thinking with the individual Christian
and consider the church as something like a social gathering or an
association of individuals sharing some common interests.*[1]

—SWISS NEW TESTAMENT SCHOLAR EDUARD SCHWEIZER
(1913–2006)

The degree to which worldliness has transformed the church is obvious
from the statistics. The incidence of such practices as abortion, pornography addiction, substance abuse, and extramarital affairs is stunning—*as
self-reported by church members.*

Across the nation, many church congregations are large and thriv-
ing, with thousands of people coming through the doors every week. Yet
commonly, church leaders don't directly address such issues as abortion,
adultery, or gambling. They fear losing members or contributions.

I have come face to face with this timidity on occasion. Some years
ago, an abortion clinic operated by Planned Parenthood opened near
one of the churches my family used to attend. Early some mornings, I
would go there and pray on the sidewalk as women arrived to take the
lives of their own children. Many saints of God would face inclement
weather and ridicule from proabortionists to take a silent stand. It felt
like being in the midst of a supernatural battle between God and Satan.

I talked with pastors about coming alongside to pray or at least visiting to see what was going on. Some did come, often weeping on their knees as they realized what they were witnessing. Others made the choice to ignore what was happening. Even though potential members were likely losing their lives just down the street from their church building, they wouldn't come, nor would they talk about it from the pulpit. Instead, they accepted murder of the innocents as the "new normal." Destabilizing the situation would be bad for their church. They were operating as a business instead of as the body of Christ.

How does it reflect on the church as a whole when so many of us gather on Sunday morning to raise our hands, sing praise and worship songs, smile, and shake hands—yet under the shampooed hair and bathed bodies, our hearts are vile? When we accept evil as the new norm?

When I talked with pastors about the abortion clinic issue, their lack of action surprised me. But I have since come to realize the underlying problem is how we view ourselves as believers. The pastors and church leaders who frustrated me were simply making rational decisions from their point of view—their church operated as a business. If church members and leaders function as members of a living body, they will tend to address deep relationship issues. However, if a church is a business, then the well-being of the business is the underlying influence when it comes to making decisions.

FADING INFLUENCE

I grew up in church after becoming a follower of Christ at the tender age of five. Ever since, I have embraced supreme confidence in the gospel. I understood that Jesus Himself established the church, His body, and gave it the task of spreading the message the world desperately needs to hear. I thought surely it would be only a matter of time until people understood this. Yet it didn't seem to work out the way I expected. Ever since my youthful decision, it seems to me the church has grown steadily less influential in the public square. This has taken place even as Christians as a whole have grown more vocal, affluent, organized, and polished.

A look at statistics helps explain why. About one-third of women attending church have had abortions. One-fourth of pastors have had an affair—while in the ministry. A whopping 76 percent of Christian young adults ages eighteen to twenty-four actively seek out porn, yet only 9 percent of churches have a program to help those struggling with pornography.[2] Spiritually speaking, we seem to be a shell of what God intends for us to be. This bothers me. What has happened? Are we not committed enough? Have we not elected enough Christians to public office? Do we lack faith? Have we not raised enough money? Authors have written thousands of books and developed countless numbers of programs to help us improve in these areas. But somehow, deep in my gut, I have always felt there must be something more basic at play.

The more I learned as a practicing physician, the more I came to view the body of Christ in biological terms: in other words, as a living body. In my opinion, the reason for our shortcomings lies in a faulty view of who we are. The way we see ourselves holds far-reaching implications for our relationships with one another. The body of Christ is not intended to function as a business or as a fraternal organization. God did not create the "business of Christ." He created the "body of Christ." He describes us in the Bible with terms associated with biology—not with business or organizational language.

In modern times, we have often become enthralled by charismatic personalities in the church. But if the body of Christ is a living body, it does not become alive and effective through the dazzling abilities or supernatural insights of individual members. This happens only through the relationships among its members.

As I studied this further, I saw two foundational errors we frequently make.

The first is to think of "the body of Christ" as just another name for the organized church. The organized church can do many good things, but it is not the body of Christ. Of course, there is overlap in member-ship between the two, but organized religion is designed to operate as an organization, not as a living body. Understanding this distinction helps explain much of the seeming feebleness of the modern-day church.

The second error is to operate the church like a business. We have tried to make the church more effective by relying on entrepreneurial expertise. Just look at the influential (and often wealthy) people asked to sit on many church boards. Generally speaking, the church has become good at raising money. We have implemented the best practices from the business world, creating well-crafted budgets and developing and executing finely tuned marketing campaigns. But how much have we relied on the Holy Spirit? Sure, we sometimes acknowledge our dependence on Jesus, but too often this means paying lip service to Christ as we decorate *our* plans with spiritual lingo. In truth, we are consumed by worldliness. We are trying to outdo the world in using the ways of the world. But the Church is intended to be in the world and not of it, to function as a living body, not as a good business. The Bible describes how we are to live using the principles of life, not the best practices from the world of business. It is past time God's Church learns to function as a body, one driven by mutual concern, love, and affection for one another. With a different outlook and philosophy, we can be the change the world is dying to find.

THE MARK OF BELIEVERS

In his short but insightful 1970 book *The Mark of the Christian*, noted apologist Francis Schaeffer observed that love toward all Christians is the identifying mark of authentic followers of Christ. It is a way to discern whether something profound has occurred to people in the spiritual realm, whether they have been transformed. They don't just *say* they are Christians; they *act* like them. In His legendary Sermon on the Mount, Jesus said, "Watch out for false prophets. They come to you in sheep's clothing, but inwardly they are ferocious wolves. *By their fruit* you will recognize them" (Matthew 7:15–16, emphasis added).

We can recognize whether people are truly following God when we identify the "mark." In a similar way, we can see what I call the "fingerprint of God" on all living creatures. This "fingerprint" refers to the identifying marks that are readily detectable after God has touched an entity and given it life. These characteristics, found in all living beings, help us to know when He has done something to them in the spiritual realm.

I am particularly interested in God's fingerprint on the Church (although not customarily capitalized, I will do so when referring to the Church as a whole rather than as an individual congregation). In terms of a living body, it is fascinating to note that the writers of the New Testament often referred to the Church in biological terms rather than in terms from business or other disciplines. Paul actually coined the term "body of Christ" to describe believers collectively. We are a living, breathing, functioning body, not a social organization or a business trying to maximize our soul-winning effectiveness.

Before we can examine God's fingerprint on the Church, we must define a term. There are several entities that go by the name *church*. Among other things, *church* can refer to a building used for Christian worship, a religious service in that building, the people who meet in that building, all Christians worldwide, a Christian denomination, or the clergy in general. This plurality of meanings can be confusing for believers and nonbelievers alike.

In this book, I will draw a distinction between *church* defined as the body of Christ and *church* defined as organized Christianity. I see the body of Christ as a living spiritual entity created by God. Because of that, it has characteristics of life—the fingerprint of God. On the other hand, people create organized Christianity to serve the body of Christ. This is not to say organized Christianity is bad, but it is not inherently good. In reality, it is neutral, because it is a tool to be used by people. And how the users subsequently wield it determines its ultimate nature.

When organized Christianity loses touch with Christianity's Christ, however, the church can take on a dark and even harmful power. Schaeffer concluded *The Mark of the Christian* by quoting the poem "Lament" by prolific poet and Irish native Evangeline Paterson:

> Weep, weep for those
> Who do the work of the Lord
> With a high look

And a proud heart.
Their voice is lifted up
In the streets, and their cry is heard.
The bruised reed they break
By their great strength, and the smoking flax
They trample.

Weep not for the quenched
(For their God will hear their cry
And the Lord will come to save them)
But weep, weep for the quenchers

For when the Day of the Lord
Is come, and the vales sing
And the hills clap their hands
And the light shines

Then their eyes shall be opened
On a waste place,
Smouldering,
The smoke of the flax bitter
In their nostrils,
Their feet pierced
By broken reed-stems . . .
Wood, hay, and stubble,
And no grass springing.
And all the birds flown.

Weep, weep for those
Who have made a desert
In the name of the Lord.[3]

Schaeffer's book and this poem serve as a cautionary warning to those who build plans and programs in God's name but don't treat others as brothers and sisters in the body of Christ. They may perform mighty works, but in the process they quench weaker believers instead of building them up in Christian love. Such self-centered souls leave a dead wasteland in their wake. The Lord will help the oppressed, but those who build themselves up without Christ's love will eventually face judgment. To survive the calamitous times ahead, we must move together in love. We are the body of Christ.

CHAPTER

1

SPIRITUAL REALITY

The spiritual world is all around us, yet almost never noticed.
It is hiding in plain sight.

I derived the above observation from years of medical experience. As a doctor, I had heard numerous stories about people who have "come back from the dead." But the events around this particular case, as the patient teetered on the precipice of eternity, sent chills down my spine.

The encounter involved a well-dressed woman in her midsixties named Mildred. She came to the emergency room (which hereafter I will refer to as the ER) after suffering from chest pains. By the time I checked her over, the staff's initial treatment had caused her pains to subside. The electrocardiogram (EKG) that checked for problems with her heart's electrical activity came back as normal. So did her vital signs.

As we waited for the results of her blood tests, I expected this would be one more routine chest pain evaluation. I had handled more than I could count. Many times, in such cases, I found no serious causes. Still, on this particular day I kept in mind the outlook I had developed over the years: namely, that the people I treat are not human machines but unique individuals with a body, a mind, and a spirit. While treating the body and the mind is fairly straightforward, the spiritual side is less easily perceived. However, when individuals are nearing their final moments on this earth, this third dimension can take on profound significance.

Not everyone sees it that way. Numerous doctors and medical personnel are accustomed to defibrillators and other technical wizardry that make it possible to literally bring people back to life. Those who trust in technology alone scoff at the idea of a spiritual reality. They attribute the phenomenon of people who once lacked a pulse drawing the breath of life again to the ordinary, everyday functioning of machinery.

But those who have lain on operating tables and experienced another dimension of the universe tell a much different story. Many describe a spiritual world that is beautiful beyond description. Some relate how they returned to this earth grudgingly because what they experienced was so wonderful they didn't want to leave. Numerous authors have written books about seeing a heaven bursting with color and awash in melodies of praise: gargantuan flowers, huge buildings, and sights and sounds no mortal can grasp with the human mind.

THE END

While some see fascinating sights and sounds, others appear tormented by the experience, like Mildred when I returned to check on her. Given my initial assurances, I expected to see my patient in a relatively calm state. Instead, agitation clouded her countenance. She glanced around the room, as if trying to find something. I gently took her hand and asked how she felt. She stared blankly toward the door to the hallway.

A minute or so later, her eyes finally flickered with recognition.

"I feel fine," she said. Then, after a long pause, she asked, "Who are they coming for? Are they coming for you?" Her question made my heart skip a beat. Turning away, she stared at an unseen entity in the distance and exclaimed with a sigh, "No. They're coming for me!" At that moment, her eyes fluttered shut. Her heart monitor flattened into a straight line.

When the heart monitor erupted with a *baaaaaaaaaaa!* I pushed the "code blue" button on the wall next to her bed. That brought a special team to the room, including respiratory therapists to give her concentrated oxygen and breathe for her, using a bag-valve-mask device. Once I placed a breathing tube into her windpipe, they turned on a ventilator and drew blood to test how well we were breathing for her.

A lab technician came to draw blood from the woman's veins and run tests for her blood counts, chemistry panel, heart enzymes, and clotting tests. An X-ray technician stood poised for a stat chest X-ray. A pair of nurses rounded out the team. One would give her medications while the other documented what we did minute by minute. She recorded such details as medications, heart monitor and oxygen level readings, blood pressure, and heart rate.

Meanwhile, I oversaw these efforts, many occurring simultaneously. I had to interpret the EKGs, heart monitor readings, lab reports, and the reports on blood gases. In addition, I had to position her head and neck in such a way as to place the breathing tube inside her trachea, using a lighted scope. This can be a difficult procedure with some patients; if not done correctly, the tube can lodge in the wrong place and cause death by suffocation. Then, I had to shock her with a defibrillator when the time came. I also had to decide which drugs to administer, by which route (intravenous line or down the breathing tube), and what dose.

We had to work as quickly and efficiently as possible. I knew the longer a patient like this was without a heartbeat, the more damage there would be to her brain and vital organs. Every second she was down meant there was less chance she would survive. As I recall this frenzied activity, it sounds heroic. But it wasn't. We worked on this patient for quite some time, but she never regained any heart rhythm or signs of life. As the emergency physician, I had to judge when to stop our efforts and pronounce her dead. That is always a subjective call, but when you have followed the ER protocols and done everything possible and there are still no signs of life, you must reach that decision.

Without a doubt, Mildred sensed something at the time of her demise—something that neither I nor the rest of the ER staff that day could see. As far as her final resting place, I don't presume to interpret what the fright on her face indicated. Yet it is difficult to experience that kind of startling event and doubt the existence of the spirit world. This experience reinforced my conviction that we were not created for a mere physical existence. The spiritual realm is as real as sunlight, a windstorm, or rain. It is as tangible as the chair in which you sit to work or relax to watch television. But it cannot be seen with the naked eye. This is one reason it is so challenging to discern the reality of the body of Christ. It exists in this spiritual dimension.

WE ARE A BODY

> Meanwhile, Saul was still breathing out murderous threats against the Lord's disciples. He went to the high priest and asked him for letters to the synagogues in Damascus, so that if he found any there who belonged to the Way, whether men or women, he might take them as prisoners to Jerusalem. As he neared Damascus on his journey, suddenly a light from heaven flashed around him. He fell to the ground and heard a voice say to him, "Saul, Saul, why do you persecute me?"
>
> "Who are you, Lord?" Saul asked.
>
> "I am Jesus, whom you are persecuting," he replied. "Now get up and go into the city, and you will be told what you must do."
>
> The men traveling with Saul stood there speechless; they heard the sound but did not see anyone. Saul got up from the ground, but when he opened his eyes he could see nothing. So they led him by the hand into Damascus. For three days he was blind, and did not eat or drink anything.
>
> —ACTS 9:1–9

The above passage describes how Jesus Christ blinded Saul (later called Paul by the Gentiles, who were his primary mission) on the road to Damascus. After restoring his vision, Christ sent him around the known world with an unknown ailment he described as a "thorn in the flesh" (see 2 Corinthians 12:7), with the physician Luke at his side. Paul used biological terms to teach that we are a living body: one body with many members, possessing all the attributes of life. And although we are individuals, in our actions, relationships, and interactions with one another—and the world—all believers are part of this body.

We learn about spiritual things that we cannot see with our eyes by comparing them to physical things that we can see. A picture is worth a thousand words; the word picture the Bible paints of the body of Christ is one as normal as our individual bodies. After all, Christ has a body that is, in some ways, similar to our physical makeup. At first, it may seem odd to compare the human body to an unseen entity, but the Bible calls God's children a body. By understanding what this means, we gain insight as to who we are from God's point of view. Studying the way the Bible uses this language can help us learn much about our unity, diversity, relationships with one another and with Christ, and our place in this world.

A BODY FIT TOGETHER

If you ask average church members, "What is the Church?" they will likely reply, "It's the body of Christ." If you follow up with: "What's the body of Christ?" they will likely answer, "It's the Church." Over time, these two terms have become interchangeable. Perhaps when it was first used, "body of Christ" was a radical idea, with world-changing implications. Yet after appearing in innumerable sermons and conversations for two thousand years, the phrase has become so familiar that for many it has taken on the character of a cliché. Its mystery and meaning have eroded. I seldom discern much awe and wonder associated with "body of Christ."

Since I grew up in church, this phrase eventually took on the flavor of religious jargon for me, too. For a long time, I didn't fully comprehend its rich implications. However, after treating many patients over the years, I find it striking that the Bible calls us a "body." That's not the first term that comes to mind when I think about Christians as a group. We may never know all the reasons that God uses it, but looking at how the human body is put together helps us know more about what He expects of us as Christians.

We are very fortunate to live in an age filled with insights about the structures and processes found in our human bodies. As a child, if someone had "cancer," I thought that automatically meant a terminal illness that left the person without hope. Today, modern medicine has learned ways to manipulate the structures and processes of our bodies so profoundly that many types of cancer and other diseases once considered a death sentence are now manageable or even curable. We are blessed to have medical technology and understanding that was unimaginable just a few years ago.

This recent explosion of medical knowledge can also be used to find a new depth of meaning in the biblical term "body." Doctors spend years studying bodies. They read volumes about human bodies, shock them back to life in the ER, operate on live ones, dissect dead ones, and see most of what can go wrong with them. Even though the inner structures and processes may not appeal to the uninitiated, there is nothing in creation more interesting. The more physicians and academicians study the way the different parts fit together, communicate with one another, and function for the body's overall benefit, the more enthralling their discoveries. There is nothing as wonderfully intricate and awe-inspiring as the human body.

BODY PARTS

If you're like me, you may feel a bit uneasy thinking of yourself as a biblical body part. However, take a deep breath, and meditate on the deeper meaning; your initial squeamishness may give way to fascination about what this means. When we take what we know scientifically about the human body and apply it to the body of Christ, we can discover deeper truths about what it means to be part of this body. As Paul wrote to the Corinthians:

> Just as a body, though one, has many parts, but all its many parts form one body, so it is with Christ. For we were all baptized by one Spirit so as to form one body—whether Jews or Gentiles, slave or free—and we were all given the one Spirit to drink. Even so the body is not made up of one part but of many. Now if the foot

should say, "Because I am not a hand, I do not belong to
the body," it would not for that reason stop being part
of the body. And if the ear should say, "Because I am
not an eye, I do not belong to the body," it would not
for that reason stop being part of the body. If the whole
body were an eye, where would the sense of hearing be?
If the whole body were an ear, where would the sense of
smell be?

—1 CORINTHIANS 12:12–17

As Paul's comparison shows, just as many parts make up our physical
bodies, so do many parts make up the body of Christ. Each person who
accepts Jesus as Savior and Lord is a member of this body. This truth
prompts me to reflect on the meaning of the phrase "body of Christ"
as it relates to our individuality. It is as individuals that we make the
decision to follow Christ. So if we come to Christ as individuals, doesn't
He deal with us individually from that moment on? This is a significant
issue, because if it is true, then the concerns of the individual will have
preeminence over the concerns of the body as a whole. Yet the church is
a body, so when God deals with me, is it as a part of the body of Christ?
Or as one person? An individualistic American male like me is more comfortable with the latter choice. Yet Scripture is clear that our Creator sees
individuals as members of a larger body—one meant to function jointly.

A multitude of souls makes up the body of Christ. We aren't self-
contained little members, with each of us commissioned to wage spiritual warfare with the enemy to win the world for Christ. None of us is
all-knowing or all-sufficient. We need one another and the perspectives
of people other than ourselves.

Each one of us is a member of the same body, with each of us playing
a unique role in its functioning. Therefore, rejection or belittling of other
members of the body should cause us pain. We should never look down
on or berate members we think to be less important than ourselves.

To me, the description of the body of Christ in the New Testament
reads more like a biology textbook than it does a business plan. Rather

than a human-led organization, we need to see ourselves as a living, divinely inspired body. So, it is helpful to use language that expresses the terms of life when speaking about this divine body.

LIVING ORGANISM

When God said that the Church is a living body, He knew that we would later discover and apply scientific facts about our physical bodies. The Bible describes the body of Christ as a living organism. While there are differences, it is amazing how many comparisons of the two appear in Scripture. Because readers of the Bible are familiar with their own bodies, it makes sense for the Word to use them as visual aids to help explain the unseen. Thinking about my own body was helpful as I learned anatomy in medical school. Otherwise, I would have been trying to wrap my mind around abstract details with no particular physical reference.

Likewise, the biblical phrase "body of Christ" helps everyone better understand the unseen spiritual world. While we live in a body, all of us have a spirit and a mind. Our body is only the temporary vehicle our spirit uses to navigate through this world. Even as it decays with age, our body serves a purpose here on earth, allowing us to interact with our external environment and others around us.

Christ, too, has a body on earth. His body serves the purpose of allowing Him to move through this physical world and interact with it. This unseen body is more real, and more detailed, than the physical bodies around us. At the time Paul wrote about the "body of Christ," the term "body" rarely referred to a group of people. Yet he used it comfortably, as if unaware of the originality of its usage. And he did it in a way that assures us he doesn't mean just "a bunch of people."

While some have called Paul's term a metaphor, I disagree. I perceive Paul as describing believers as individual members of an entity that is an actual, living organism. The apostle saw the body of Christ as a kind of realm into which individuals must enter in order to reach their purpose and be fully alive in Christ. Paul also described the church in other ways, like "flock," "wife," "temple," or "family"—words with roots in the Old

17

Testament. However, this isn't true of the phrase "body of Christ." From a Hebrew language perspective, it seems that Paul produced this term from nowhere. The Hebrew believers in the first-century church who read his letters had to be more than a little surprised.

The bridge between the Old Testament thinking of believers as a "building" or "temple" and the new term "body of Christ" appears in John, where Jesus referred to the "temple" and the "body" as one and the same: "Jesus answered them, 'Destroy this temple, and I will raise it again in three days.' They replied, 'It has taken forty-six years to build this temple, and you are going to raise it in three days?' But the temple he had spoken of was his body. After he was raised from the dead, his disciples recalled what he had said. Then they believed the scripture and the words that Jesus had spoken" (John 2:19–22).

When Jesus became a man and walked on earth, He was constrained by His bodily limitations. Today, things are different. The body of Christ is, in effect, present at all times and in every place across the world. Jesus is constrained now only by the limitations of the body of Christ instead of those of His earthly body. He does nothing on earth separate from the body, and the body can do nothing separate from Him. Perhaps He was addressing us as a body, rather than as individuals, when He said: "Very truly I tell you, whoever believes in me will do the works I have been doing, and they will do even greater things than these, because I am going to the Father" (John 14:12).

SYMBOLS AND MEANING

"Man, as we realize if we reflect for a moment, never perceives anything fully or comprehends anything completely."[1]
—SWISS PSYCHIATRIST CARL G. JUNG

The way people use language provides insight into their thought processes. The ancient Hebrews thought of the "body" in a different way than we do today. We emphasize the autonomy of the individual; they saw themselves as a collective "flesh." The question Westerners must ask ourselves is whether we can understand the Hebraic meaning. Has our worldview become too individualistic and self-centered? Over time, we have progressed from not considering the individual body to almost worshiping it. This is probably the main obstacle to our understanding of the body of Christ. We are believers tainted by the spirit of a narcissistic age.

We use verbal symbols, or words, to communicate our ideas with others. But in using such symbols, there will always be a slight difference in meaning between what the speaker intends to communicate and what the hearer understands. This isn't just because people don't listen. Differences in background, education, and life experiences can put a different interpretation on the same words. In fact, different people have slightly varying definitions of the same word. Thus, another person usually gets the gist of what we're saying, but as Carl Jung observed, we never achieve 100 percent correlation. For practical, everyday interactions, what people lose in the process is not a major problem. However, when we need to communicate in precise terminology, this can pose significant problems.

These problems are rooted in the way we use symbols, which are like containers (I picture them as bowls) holding meanings. They have the power to shape how we understand our world and ourselves. When we have symbols that are true to God's plan for us, we can enjoy their richness as we fulfill His purpose for our lives. For example, we can endure incredible hardship if we understand its meaning.

Again, "body of Christ" is probably not symbolic or metaphorical, but rather literal. We are not *like* the body of Christ; we *are* the body of Christ. The concept is not one of multiple personalities in community but of a single organism with a single personality.

In his letter to the Romans, Paul wrote that "in Christ we, though many, form one body, and each member belongs to all the others" (Romans 12:5). At that time, any other writer might have written that "we, though many, are one body," which would have emphasized the unity of the believers. But Paul added the crucial phrase "in Christ," which helps us know that we are to be more than just unified in the same way our favorite football team, sorority, or fraternal organization comes together to achieve a particular goal.

The Whole Is Greater Than the Sum of the Parts

I believe Paul taught that when we become believers, we are to see ourselves primarily as the body of Christ and only in a secondary sense as individual members. The ancient Greek philosopher Aristotle is credited with originating this familiar phrase passed on by numerous observers: "the whole is greater than the sum of the parts." This is true of the body of Christ. The whole body is greater than the sum of the individual members, because the Spirit of Christ arises in our midst. The essence of the body of Christ is derived from the interactions among the members, not from the individual members themselves. Otherwise, the church is just a gathering of individuals with common interests.

How did Paul get such a novel idea as to equate Christian people with Jesus Christ? Maybe part of the answer comes from his encounter with Christ on the road to Damascus. When a light from heaven flashed around him and Paul fell to the ground, Jesus inquired, "Why are you persecuting Me?" Notice that Jesus didn't ask, "Why are you persecuting My people?" Paul's initial, life-changing encounter with Christ cemented this connection forever in his mind. It prompted him to write the words from 1 Corinthians 12:12 that I quoted earlier in this chapter: "Just as a body, though one, has many parts, but all its many parts form one body, so it is with Christ." The ending to that sentence is a key to understanding the importance of the body. Paul didn't end with the words "so it is with the church." Instead, he wrote "so it is with Christ." This shows how deeply Paul felt we are one with Christ, and not unified individuals.

It is vital to keep the meaning clear in our minds and hearts. The body of Christ is clearly defined in the Bible. The body is composed of individual believers—nothing more. So, local churches, ministry organizations, denominations, Christian music, Christian literature, and Christian schools do good things and serve worthwhile purposes, but they are not part of the body. Although useful for assisting us in accomplishing God's plans, neither Christian organizations nor church institutions are part of the body. It consists of individual believers.

Jesus did not only create and found the church; He is still present in the church and gives it life. When we are healthy members of the body of Christ, we can participate in the same life and power that motivated our Savior when He walked on this earth. Jesus makes Himself known more fully to us as a body than to us as individuals. Only a living spiritual organism can fulfill the plan of God for the world; many religious organizations have tried and failed. The first step to succeeding is to see ourselves as the body of Christ.

QUESTIONS FOR DISCUSSION

1. Have you ever meditated on the body of Christ being a living body? How do you think a living body is different from a business or an organization?

2. Each person accepts Christ as an individual. Do you think Christ deals with us as individual believers, all together, or both? Explain.

3. What does it mean that Jesus does nothing on earth separate from the body, and the body can do nothing separate from Him?

4. Do you think believers are just "like" a living body or that they truly are a living body? Why?

5. In the body of Christ, the "whole is greater than the sum of the parts." What do you think this means? How have you seen this played out in daily life?

6. Is it the qualities of individual members that give a body its essence, or is it the interactions among the members? What does this say about the importance of relationships in the body of Christ?

7. What is the body of Christ comprised of? Is your church denomination part of this body?

CHAPTER
2

THE VISION

When the church is the church . . . the people of God
moved by the Spirit of God do the work of God, and
evil cannot stand against them. That is the mandate
Jesus put before His followers centuries ago.[1]
—**CHARLES COLSON, FOUNDER OF PRISON FELLOWSHIP**

When the Church fails to realize it is actually the body of Christ and its
members are in unity, the body of Christ becomes sick. Although more
than three decades have passed, a friend still feels the emotional sting left
by a contentious church business meeting. On that Wednesday night, a
contingent of strange faces showed up determined to vote out the pastor.
The church, which shall remain nameless, was of the congregationally
governed variety. Since membership had never been clearly defined or
enforced, those who claimed membership status could typically do so
unchallenged, even if they hadn't darkened the doors for several years.

"Looking back, I guess it's a wonder that we didn't simply walk out
the door and never come back to any church," my friend says. "At the
time, we had only been Christians for about two years. The ugliness
displayed that night is one of those memories that will stay with me
forever. People who claimed to follow Jesus were anything but loving.
They were bullheaded, opinionated, stubborn, and self-righteous."

My friend and his wife wound up later leaving that church; the pastor
proved to be unreliable and dishonest, claiming to know the Bible inside
and out while often displaying unfamiliarity with its teachings. Still,
that night, my friends wondered why people who had never shown up

to stem the exodus that followed the resignation of the previous pastor suddenly cared so much about who occupied the pulpit. Their numbers included individuals who had stopped coming during the past year, as well as a number of faces they had never seen. For such absentees to claim "voting membership" struck my friend as absurd.

The session raged for more than ninety minutes. Tempers flared, the volume of voices ratcheted ever higher, and one man who pleaded for understanding and charity was largely ignored. The pastor outfoxed his detractors by never calling the meeting to order. At one point, he defused an attack by breaking a confidence and revealing that he had offered marital counseling to a couple siding with the "oust the pastor" faction. Needless to say, they never returned. Neither did the rest of the naysayers. While the pastor temporarily blocked his ouster, that church wound up fizzling into nothingness.

LOVING THE CHURCH

It doesn't matter where this meeting happened or in what denomination. Similar stories abound, regardless of background or doctrinal beliefs. Too often, people who are instructed to love everyone—even their enemies—display little evidence of a compassionate heart.

However, it isn't church splits that are the problem. They simply provide evidence of a more deeply rooted crisis: a failure to love the body of Christ. I don't mean the kind of intrachurch squabbles I just described, or quarrels about the color of the carpet or what paint is used for the kitchen (arguments that sound silly but symbolize deep-rooted struggles over power, prestige, or position). I'm talking about the brickbats that often get thrown between different factions within denominations, or at members of other denominations, or between broad-based groups of believers: "Well, those Baptists . . ." "You can't believe anything those Pentecostals say . . ." "It's those Catholics . . ."

Noted pastor and author Rick Warren addressed this sad condition once on his Facebook page, observing that too many Christians use the church but don't love it. That is something he says is hard for many of us to hear: "We've been deeply hurt by members of the church, we've been disappointed, we can be discouraged. But the Church is the bride of Christ. It's the hope of the world, the vessel through which God works out his plan. We have to learn to love the church. For some of us that means there's people we need to forgive, for others it means we need to get involved in service, and for others it means we need to change how we talk of the church. Jesus loves his church. If for no other reason than that—we must love the church also."[2]

I wholeheartedly echo Warren's sentiment, which reflects a truth that God wants us to understand about the spiritual world. As I said in the first chapter, the body of Christ is real, not just a metaphor. It is a living spiritual entity that God created just as He created all other living things on earth.

The body of Christ is not just a "good idea" or a "good option." It is the *only* option, the plan God created to fulfill His will on earth. When Jesus asked His disciples who others thought the Son of Man was, they responded that the guesses ranged from John the Baptist to Elijah or Jeremiah. Christ wanted to know, though, what they thought. When Peter replied that He was the Messiah, the Son of the living God, Jesus answered, "Blessed are you, Simon son of Jonah, for this was not revealed to you by flesh and blood, but by my Father in heaven. And I tell you that you are Peter, and on this rock I will build my church, and the gates of Hades [meaning hell] will not overcome it" (Matthew 16:17–18). The Church is Jesus's secret weapon in the eternal battle between good and evil that has raged in the heavens throughout eternity, before even the creation of our planet.

BEING THE CHURCH

In order for the Church to prevail against the forces of evil, however, its members must not only *love* the Church, we must *be* the Church. Sadly, the personality and traits of our culture are too often reflected in our local churches. We live in a society that emphasizes the superficial. What amazes me is how, instead of rejecting the idea that appearance is the leading measure of value, church members too frequently reflect this pattern. I know an evangelist who has marveled at how many beautiful couples from his Bible college days are now divorced because they chose a spouse based primarily on appearance. Over the years, I have also met numerous church members who selected a marriage partner according to the most transient and superficial of qualities and then wondered why they fell out of love and saw their marriage dissolve.

The breakdown of Christian marriages is one indication that we modern believers are too enticed by shallow matters. We promote dazzling events to draw large crowds without considering whether we are making a lasting impact on the world. My vision for the body of Christ is for it to be an effective influence on society. While churches are sometimes dysfunctional and ineffective organizations, this does not need to be a permanent condition.

The essential purpose of the Church is not merely to perform nice programs at 11:00 on Sunday mornings but to be salt and light in our society. Indeed, we should make this our overarching goal. While that may seem like a revolutionary concept, we in fact are in need of a revolution. We need a paradigm shift—not just a trim around the edges of the status quo or a fine-tuning of our services to make them *a little more interesting* and welcoming to newcomers. We must have revival, and it must begin in our hearts. I believe the current tensions between the church and society will continue to grow until there is some sort of tectonic upheaval. Will this conflict lead us into great revival, or will the organized church be persecuted into oblivion? I pray that the body of Christ will summon its courage and take the initiative to lead the way. We have a great opportunity.

While I don't believe in living in the past or lamenting that things aren't the way they used to be, in the twenty-first century we must ask ourselves whether the Church in our generation is as successful a witness to the world as was the first-century Church. That early-day Church came about in a very unreceptive, wicked society—even more so than our own. Paul's letters to the church at Corinth address such practices as a man openly living with his father's wife, pagan sacrifices offered to demons, the worship of false gods, and prostitution.

So today, we must ask ourselves such questions as:

- Are we a vibrant, world-changing force like the early Church?
- Does the world find us pertinent at all? If not, then why not?
- What is necessary for us to be effective once more as salt and light in our world?

Many have suggested remedies for our ineffectiveness. Some have proven useful, at least for a while. But I am proposing that, when it comes to increasing the impact of the twenty-first century Church, the key will not come from changing what we do or how we do it. Instead, the answer lies in how we see ourselves. It demands leaving behind the idea that Christianity involves a "Jesus and me" relationship. We are many members in one body.

This is the paradigm shift to which I referred earlier. "Church" is not just a building in which we do Christian things. We must recognize that, no matter where we live, work, or travel, the Church is to present the body of Christ.

THE MOST IMPORTANT THING

Physicians usually think about problems in terms of diagnosis and treatment. As a long-time Christian, I have also given considerable thought to the problems facing the modern Church and how we have tried to address them. Consider the abundance of treatment options available to help the church become more effective. We have church-growth programs, staff-development programs, evangelism-training seminars, fundraising drives, conferences, workshops, and revival meetings. While these remedies are appropriate at times, if we are to take action like good physicians (rather than quacks) do, we must determine the best treatment by first looking at the underlying, eternal issues.

Such contemplation and action is necessary for the long-term health of the Church. If we concentrate only on immediate troubles and discomforts, we will set ourselves up for a never-ending succession of problems requiring repeated attention. Fortunately, God has a plan for the long-term health and well-being of the Church. It doesn't rely on human wisdom. It's called being the body of Christ.

The urgent situation facing the Church is not a need to change what we do so much as it is a need to know who we are. Relying on things like the aforementioned conferences, seminars, and revivals means we fix short-term problems. This is akin to relieving the pain a cancer patient feels without changing the underlying disease process. When we understand that we are the body of Christ, our path to long-term health and effectiveness becomes possible. The success of the body of Christ does not depend on the number of people involved; it depends on the Spirit of God. In the end, it is God and not us who has the power to make the body of Christ successful.

I have come to conclude that—in spiritual terms—the body of Christ is the most important entity in the world. It is the instrument God created to save mankind, wage war with the devil and his forces of evil, provide healing, and complete the good works of God in our world. In addition, I believe too many Christians misunderstand and underappreciate the body of Christ's strategic importance. Although we know it is mentioned in the Bible, we can easily pass it off as a sort of strange metaphor. Its meaning can become muddled as we are distracted by the challenges of everyday life.

We often seek a Christianity that focuses on us as individuals and brings us wealth and comfort. This is a profound distortion of God's plan. If we fail to grasp the importance of the body and our importance to one another for persevering through the challenges of life in this world, we miss the mark. That is why I feel so strongly about the need for an increased understanding of the body of Christ.

A wise man once said that the more he learned, the less he seemed to know. I frequently feel the same way as I study how the Bible uses "body of Christ" to describe us. There is a wealth of meaning to be discovered in this term. However, the more I learn, the more questions I find that need to be answered. I think I am straining to grasp the picture about which Paul wrote in the famous "love" chapter in 1 Corinthians: "For we know in part and we prophesy in part, but when completeness comes, what is in part disappears. When I was a child, I talked like a child, I thought like a child, I reasoned like a child. When I became a man, I put the ways of childhood behind me. For now we see only a reflection as in a mirror; then we shall see face to face. Now I know in part; then I shall know fully, even as I am fully known" (1 Corinthians 13:9–12).

In the pages to come, I will consider what it means if we take this thought seriously: that we *really are* a living body, representing God's love and activity in the world.

QUESTIONS FOR DISCUSSION

1. Do you agree that many people use the Church but don't love it? What does this suggest about our understanding of the Church?
2. Besides the body of Christ, what other options did God create to fulfill His will on earth?
3. Are we a vibrant, world-changing force like the early Church in Acts? Why do you say that?
4. Do you think the world finds the Church pertinent? If not, then why not?
5. What is necessary for us to be effective once more as salt and light in our world?
6. Do you feel our weaknesses stem from not doing the right things in church? Or do they stem from how we view ourselves? Explain.

CHAPTER
3

BODIES

*It was Martin Buber who once observed that the Hebrew
first sees the woods and only then single trees; whereas we in
the Western world would see first the single tree, and only after
a process of reflection do we call a thousand trees a wood.
We Western people really miss the woods for the trees.*[1]

—EDUARD SCHWEIZER

During my residency training, I spent several months caring for hospital
patients. Every morning, our entourage of five or six doctors, residents,
and students in white coats went from room to room to check on patients
assigned to our medical team. One lady who stands out in memory is
Donna Sue. She suffered from pneumonia, but her long-term problem
originated with her battles with weight. Although she was seemingly on
the mend from pneumonia, antibiotics and other medications weren't
going to cure her morbid obesity. Therefore, we did our best to help her
shed excessive weight, placing her on a strict diet while she recuperated.
We emphasized the medical necessity of this regimen and why this calor-
ic restriction was necessary for her future health and well-being.

Yet, after several days of this strict diet, we were confounded to discover it wasn't working. If anything, Donna Sue seemed to have added a
few pounds. So, we set out to search for a myriad of rarely seen metabolic
causes behind this problem. On this particular day, I went to check her
heart and lungs, trying to tactfully lift the rolls of fat before placing my
stethoscope onto her chest. To my surprise, a flattened Twinkie—still
encased in its clear wrapper—fell from somewhere in the folds of her

torso and landed on her bedsheets. We discovered she had been sending a friend to the candy machine for goodies. No wonder!

For years, I've prescribed various treatments for sick people. Like my overweight patient, some ignore the therapies that could help them regain their health. As a longtime follower of Christ, I have a similar concern for what I see as ineffective treatments for ills in the Church (particularly in America). Many books have been written about how to help the Church. But many of the treatments prescribed assume the church should be operated as a business. Indeed, we often do run the church that way. Like a corporation in a proxy battle, we line up voting members to support our interests. We compete for control of the church. In place of evangelism, we have marketing campaigns. The senior pastor is our CEO, and elders are our board of directors. Clergy and laity are separate from each another, occupying separate turf and not crossing into each other's fiefdoms. We try to win the world by using the ways of the world and then wonder why in the world we are irrelevant when we step outside the church walls.

The fact that we're a living body has largely been lost. This is reflected by how little I discovered during my readings about the biological or "living" point of view of church life. Why is this so? I believe that as our society has grown more affluent, believers have self-organized local churches using a business model instead of a living-body model. This seems practical on multiple fronts: projects must be serviced, operating expenses paid, people in charge held accountable, and the church made presentable to the community. Wanting to avoid the cultish image of snake handlers or chandelier swingers, we become like small businesses: efficient, sensible, and good stewards of all that God provided.

Ironically, I have found more emphasis on the biological concept, which is so vital for a healthy church, in secular material than in books written by Christian writers. Business authors understand the value of biological concepts. These books suggest businesses work better when they feature biological (i.e., "organic") designs rather than the top-down control design rooted in the early days of the Industrial Age—the one that seems popular in too many sanctuaries.

The frustrating aspect is that while church people often don't "get it," highly intelligent people in the world do (even though they may use different terminologies and have little to say about the Church). Whether they are organizational leaders, business managers, game theorists, or computer programmers, smart people recognize that mimicking biological principles works. It works because that's how God made living things, with all sorts of positive developments that would be impossible without a living model. However, the Church—which is supposed to be a living body—has moved in the opposite direction. This is disastrous, because the Church is under ever-increasing attack. As subtle attacks turn into less-veiled hostility and persecution increases, believers will need to understand they are members of a living body and not just part of a church establishment that can be usurped or driven out of business by worldly powers.

DIVINE IMPRINT

I learned something about how the body of Christ works by studying the human body. It's not that the human body is a reflection of the body of Christ or that the body of Christ is a reflection of the human body. They possess similarities because both reflect the nature of the God who made them.

Growing up, I assumed that the Bible called believers a body as a way of describing them as a group. In the same way you might consider a lake a "body of water" containing countless drops of liquid, I thought "body of Christ" represented a good way to mentally group Christians together. As I learned more about the science of living bodies, though, I came to understand that God intended us to be much more than a random collection of individuals. He created us to be a living entity—not an organization. Created by God, the Church should exhibit characteristics of life similar to those of other living organisms.

Two words central to this issue are "organism" and "organization." They differ in several respects. People *cannot* create living things, or organisms. They *can* fashion organizations (that are not living) as a means to reach goals. I'm not opposed to organizations; when used to organize people to complete good deeds, they can accomplish much.

Still, organizations are made by people and aren't alive. We should not fall into the trap of thinking of the body of Christ as a man-made organization; it is a living organism created by the hand of God. In John's apocryphal vision in Revelation, he described the twenty-four elders falling down before Christ and laying their crowns before His throne with these words: "You are worthy, our Lord and God, to receive glory and honor and power, for you created all things, and by your will they were created and have their being" (Revelation 4:11).

God alone creates life and all the living things that have ever existed. God breathed life into Adam and placed him in the garden to be a steward and walk in relationship with Him. He created all living plants and animals. Likewise, He created the body of Christ and gave life to it. Christians are intended to exist in this world as a living organism, not as a nonliving organization.

While some Scriptures compare Christians to other living plants or animals, in this book I will compare the body of Christ to the human body. This is partly because of my medical background but also because the Bible so often uses the human body as an illustration.

THE ARTIST'S SIGNATURE

Art connoisseurs can confidently determine what artist created a particular piece, even without an identifying signature or label. They simply observe the painting's style and physical attributes. The same is true of music aficionados. They can frequently discern the composer of a musical piece by finding characteristics that run as a thread throughout the composer's work. These threads can be considered that composer's "fingerprint" on his or her work.

Likewise, because the same God who created all other living things fashioned the body of Christ, we may look for a thread of similar qualities in His work. I like to think of these shared characteristics as God's fingerprint on His creation. The nature of the Creator may be found as we examine His fingerprint on all living things. The true nature and purpose of the church may become clearer through comparison with other living things around us.

The Bible records simple stories, or parables, that Jesus told in order to teach spiritual lessons. The illustrations often involve physical objects we experience in everyday life. These parables are clear and effective because the Creator's fingerprint is on the things He creates, whether seen or unseen. We can visualize and better understand unseen spiritual things if we study the characteristics common to familiar, physical objects that we can see. By examining the characteristics of life found in living things, we can see how these same features are woven into God's plan for relationships in the body of Christ. Scientifically speaking, things that have these attributes are alive; things that aren't alive do not. God intends for the body of Christ to be a living organism and have qualities of life.

LIVING ATTRIBUTES

Let us examine some of the attributes of living bodies—characteristics that scientists identify as essential for life. They can be used to differentiate between what is alive and what is not. So if the body of Christ is living, we should be able to find them in the church. They include:

1. **Movement**

   All living bodies have movement. But movements aren't always visible to the naked eye. There are movements deep inside the body—some so miniscule as to be detected only with the aid of a microscope. Did you know that, even when you're at rest, your body displays movement? Blood moves through your arteries and veins. Likewise, small substances inside the cells of your body are constantly in motion. Plants don't usually move externally from place to place. (Some call this *locomotion* rather than *movement*.) Still, living plants have constant movement of substances inside their cells and throughout their texture because movement is an essential characteristic of living things.

2. **Vital Resources**

   All living things require a constant supply of energy and other resources. This allows them to carry out the processes of life and manufacture the substances needed by their cells. Because living things need a constant flow of energy to remain alive, they usually store extra energy for future use. The human body stores energy in fat cells for later use.

All living things use resources to maintain the structures and processes in the body. The intricate processes within a living body are in a dynamic yet balanced state of flux called homeostasis. Living bodies cannot survive in a stagnant, unchanging state because the environment around them changes constantly. They must adjust to these changes to preserve their internal stability. When a living organism no longer has the resources it needs, its molecules fall into disorder. Death rapidly ensues.

3. **Growth and Development**

All living things grow and develop. Nonliving entities may undergo addition, but they do not grow and develop in the way living things do. Curious as a youngster about science and nature, I would dissolve sugar in water and let the water evaporate to form rock candy. The rock candy could increase in size when material was added to it, but it was not alive. Growth is an essential process identified in living organisms. Interestingly, some living things grow without increasing in size at all. They mature and grow through the process of assimilation, whereby they take in food and transform it into living tissue.

Just like other living bodies, the body of Christ has growth. Sometimes we describe church growth as the process of adding people to our congregation's membership rolls. But that is addition—not the growth of a living body. Growth in the living body of Christ includes the spiritual development of individual members to the point that they are mature enough to produce and disciple other believers. Every living body requires some sort of food for energy. Knowing this, Jesus feeds and cares for His body, ensuring adequate nutrition for growth and development.

4. Reproduction

All living things reproduce. They reproduce at the cellular level by growing new cells to replace old, worn-out cells. An individual cell does this by splitting into multiple cells. Nonliving things can be divided but can't reproduce. A rock can be divided into two halves by striking it with a sledgehammer, but the two halves cannot become like the original rock. The rock cannot produce offspring. When the body of Christ is studied, the difference between splitting and reproducing is an important distinction. A church plant could be equated to the latter, whereas a congregational or denominational split would be indicative of a human disagreement within an organization.

5. Biogenesis

All life comes from preexisting life. The word scientists use for this is "biogenesis."

In the living body of Christ, this ever-changing life springs from the lives of our predecessors. Hebrews 12:1 calls them "a great cloud of witnesses."

6. Cells

All living things are made from cells. They are the building blocks used to construct a living body. Some of the smallest organisms, such as bacteria, have only one cell and are so small they cannot be seen with the naked eye. Others are so large they contain billions of cells. However, whether large or small, all living things utilize the cell as their basic structural and functional unit. Cells within a living body have various sizes and shapes, depending on what they are called on to do for the organism. The size of an organism doesn't indicate the size of its cells. Instead, it signifies the number of cells composing it. When a cell reaches a certain level of maturity, it is natural for it to divide into two new cells. Each possesses the characteristics of the parent cell. This reproductive process can occur only when a cell's internal infrastructure is capable of dividing into two self-supporting cells.

7. **Adaptation**

All living bodies are able to adjust to changing situations. Scientists call this "adaptation." Every member of the body is able to change its functions as required for the overall good of the body. These changes are necessary according to the season, the time, or the demands placed on the body by its environment. This is part of the dynamic nature of a living body. When the body of Christ is healthy, it can adjust and adapt and yet maintain orthodoxy.

8. **Unity amid Diversity**

All living bodies exhibit both unity and diversity among their members. A living body can't exist in uniformity throughout, like a jug of homogenized milk, in which the last sip tastes the same as the first. For it to live, a body must have many different kinds of members playing various roles. If a body consisted of identical parts, it could not function properly. While there might be few conflicts among its members, this wouldn't signal unity. Lack of conflict may project a superficial calmness and stability. If the lack of conflict stems from a lack of diversity among the members, though, the body dies.

The members of the body must be different to support life. But a body also needs clear vision and leadership to keep its members focused on the higher calling and not on "doing their own thing." There must be both diversity and unity. Because of our innate human proclivity to seek out others like ourselves, many Christians display a tendency to want others in the body of Christ to look and act just as they do. They want to make others conform to their own religious concepts. But God didn't create us to be identical. We all have similarities, but we're each unique. This diversity makes for a healthy body. Blood is meant to flow, not harden, just as bones are meant to harden, not flow. The body needs members with a range of abilities to be healthy.

Because we are members of a body, none of us is complete alone. This is why the Creator makes each of us so unique; He forces us to need one another. Hence, we not only need to tolerate diversity within the body of Christ, we need to promote it. Living bodies are highly organized and have both diversity and unity among their members.

9. Written Guidelines

All living things have a written set of guidelines by which its members live. This is the genetic code found in DNA. The guidelines for members of the body of Christ are written in the Bible.

10. Turnover of Body Members

All living things die and return to dust. Indeed, cells of living things constantly die and are replaced through the process of growth. A living body remains alive by expending large amounts of energy to replace dying cells. The dynamic nature of life is underscored by the way we are born into this world yet eventually die and return to dust. Our human bodies are mortal. God makes us this way as a gentle reminder that this world is not our home. This is His way of coaxing us into the body of Christ.

SICKNESS IN THE BODY

The Church is a living body, and like a living body, it can sometimes get sick. Living bodies remain in good health as long as their component parts are healthy. But disease can develop when the parts are not functioning well or if the interactions among them become destructive. We can look at similarities between disease processes—like immune system problems, infection, and cancer—in our natural bodies and the dysfunctions that affect the body of Christ. By seeing how these problems occur in our natural bodies, we can better understand how to identify and correct problems in the body of Christ. Just as the natural body has a profound ability to heal itself, the body of Christ is equipped with biblical mechanisms to bring about healing among its members.

We can learn from science and Scripture how God created living bodies to function. Then we will be able to understand the most common sicknesses in the life of the body of Christ, such as lack of forgiveness, lack of discernment, and lack of charity. You may say: "These are not diseases!" Not in the classical sense. But after learning about living organisms from a biblical perspective, it is easy to understand how problems found in the body of Christ parallel medical conditions, such as:

1. **Lack of Forgiveness**

    In the body of Christ, lack of forgiveness is like a disease of the immune system. If you have an immune disease, such as rheumatoid arthritis or lupus, think of how much pain and disability result from one part of your body judging other parts as not being part of the same body and attacking them. When we—as members of the body of Christ—attack one another, it is devastating for the cause of Christ.

2. **Lack of Discernment**

    Lack of discernment is like infection in the human body. When the culture of the world invades the church, it leads members astray. It is like an infection that festers and eventually makes the entire body sick and weak.

3. **Lack of Charity**

    Lack of charity is a disease process in the body of Christ that behaves like cancer. When you have cancer, one cell—or group of cells—has decided to build itself up at the expense of others, even if the resulting imbalance destroys your health—or even kills you. So it is when a person in the body of Christ thinks of himself, or herself, more highly than they ought. This lack of charity destroys relationships with other members of the body and ultimately causes it to have terrible pain and disability.

Fortunately, the Great Physician has provided a manual for treatment and healing in the body of Christ. Namely, the Bible. We can look at what is written in Scripture and apply it as we do our part to be members of a healthy, living body.

The body of Christ has often been weak and ineffective in spite of the energy and resources of its members. This is partially because of a flawed self-image. While we have done our best to be a great organization, the church can be effective and accomplish its purpose in this world only if we form a living organism. We can't accomplish this through man-made organizations, no matter how good they may be.

I have discovered that when people are sick and hurting, they tend to focus internally on themselves and their circumstances. This is a natural tendency; after all, when we're sick, we need to pay attention to getting things back in balance. Still, when it comes to the body of Christ, it is healthier to look outside of ourselves and see the big picture by taking a view from God's perspective. This is what I hope to accomplish: to focus on our place in the body of Christ and what that means in terms of health and healing. After all, as I noted in chapter 2, the body of Christ is not just a good idea. It is God's one and only plan for us.

QUESTIONS FOR DISCUSSION

1. How has a biological model helped businesses become more successful?
2. Jesus taught many lessons through parables. Is there a particular physical example in the Bible that has helped you better understand the spiritual dimension of life? Explain.
3. If the body of Christ is a living body, what are some of the attributes of life we should be able to identify in the Church?
4. What is the difference between "growth" and "addition" in the church? What would growth mean to you?
5. How can a living body have unity and diversity at the same time?
6. How does lack of forgiveness in the body of Christ resemble diseases of the immune system? Have you ever experienced this?

7. How does lack of discernment in the body of Christ resemble infection? Have you ever experienced this?

8. How does lack of charity in the body of Christ resemble cancer? Have you ever experienced this?

9. Why can't man-made organizations accomplish God's plan for mankind?

CHAPTER
4

ARE WE A BODY OR A BUSINESS?

*What do I mean by organism? The church in its most
fundamental essence is nothing less than an interdependent,
life-pulsating people who are indwelled by the presence
of a resurrected and reigning Christ.*[1]
—**PASTOR GREG OGDEN, AUTHOR OF** *UNFINISHED BUSINESS*

One of the first patients I ever treated was a woman who showed up at
the ER with abdominal pain. Mrs. Gonzales was a difficult patient to
examine, and not just because of my lack of experience. Her large girth
would have challenged a veteran physician. To her surprise, we discovered that she wasn't suffering from gastritis, indigestion, or an abdominal
ailment at all; she was pregnant. To my surprise, we also discovered the
baby was ready to be delivered immediately. And I hadn't even graduated
from medical school yet!

This experience took place during my third year of medical school.
After four years of college and two more years of medical lectures, my
fellow students and I had been given real live patients to treat. This
represented an enormous change in our everyday lives. No longer did we
focus just on attending lectures and passing exams. I was both excited
and terrified. (I can only imagine what it felt like for the patients.)

Somehow, my patient hadn't realized that nine months of bloat-
ing and weight gain had stemmed from her pregnancy. While I felt
a youthful impulse to ask how this situation had developed *without
her knowledge*, a more urgent task demanded my attention: delivering
the baby. Not only had I treated just a handful of patients, but I had

never even observed a delivery. It was time for a review—and fast. I quickly located my obstetrics textbook and reread the "labor and delivery" section as the contractions of a previously unnoticed pregnancy progressed in the background. The phrase "the blind leading the blind" came to mind.

Considering my lack of experience, the delivery went relatively smoothly. The main thing I had to remember was to not drop the baby (which isn't as easy as it sounds; it can be akin to grasping a slippery bar of soap). Both the patient and I felt relief after the infant had fully emerged from the birth canal. However, my heart quickly sank when I saw the little boy's lack of movement and bluish hue and mistakenly thought I had killed him during the ordeal. Thankfully, a few seconds later, he started breathing and squirming. Later, I learned it's not uncommon for newly delivered babies to require some gentle stimulation before they inhale air at full capacity and turn their deathly tint into a lively pink.

A VITAL ORGANISM

As a medical student, I was still learning how to deliver a baby. I needed my textbook and assistance to know what to do before I could help Mrs. Gonzales deliver her son. Just as additional training, education, and practice helped me learn the art of bringing children into the world, believers can learn how to function as the body of Christ through the instructions given in the Bible and interaction with their fellow members.

As I mentioned in chapter 2, the body of Christ is a living organism created by God. And like any other animal or plant, it exhibits the attributes of life I reviewed in chapter 3.

A key point is that God makes organisms. Because mankind also has a creative bent, men and women are good at forming organizations. While those can be quite useful, they don't necessarily possess the characteristics of a living organism. I have a friend who—if he senses an idea is from the mind of God—says: "That has life on it." Through closer inspection, we can discern whether something has the properties of life.

Let's start with an examination of some familiar terms: partnerships, teams, and machines.

While "body of Christ" has assumed cliché status in many segments of the church, if you meditate on the idea for a while, you will appreciate the fact that several terms for Christians are less disturbing and consequential. Familiar, comfortable terms tend to picture us as an organization rather than as a living organism. Ask church members to describe how modern Christians are put together, and they might use such phrases as "partners bonded together for Christ," "teammates on the Christian team," or maybe even "employees of an organization for Christ."

However, the Bible doesn't use these nonliving descriptions for us. Now, it is true there are partners in the Bible. Paul and Luke were partners in the book of Acts, and Jesus sent out His disciples in groups of two. Still, when the Bible discusses our role as Christians, it describes us as members of the body of Christ. This is not a casual association. "Body" implies a lifelong, tight-knit relationship that is much more difficult to break than is a partnership. Cut a hand from the body, and the trauma is long lasting. The same is true for a toe. Break any bone, no matter how large or small, and the anguish is immediate for the entire body.

OK, so why not describe us as teammates? It seems fitting, and thanks to the popularity of such sports as football, millions are familiar with the concept. I remember the preacher who frequently used the analogy of a team moving the football down the field against spiritual enemies. I have also heard people describe members of their local church (or believers in general) as teammates. Former pastor Greg Ogden, whose quote opened this chapter, said of team ministry: "In the hierarchical structure the senior pastor's role is very much like the football coach who assigns the players on their position and calls the plays that are going to be run on the field. The staff knows clearly that their roles are defined for the efficient operation of the organization according to the senior pastor's perception of the needs of the congregation."[2]

Ultimately, though, teams are still organizations. Being part of a living body requires relationships more intimate than those shared by teammates. The coach can substitute one player for another much more easily than a body can substitute one member for another, especially when spiritual gifts vary from person to person. A team exerts more pressure toward conformity, which is why teammates may be thought of as being interchangeable. A team member is a fully functioning, living unit independent of the team. But a member of a spiritual body cannot live for long unless it remains a part of the body.

In addition, a body is more dependent on vision and leadership for success than is a team. For example, a sports team might succeed when all the teammates play their best as individuals and give 100 percent. That isn't necessarily true of the body of Christ; we are created to be more unified as a single unit than a team of individuals is. Our success is built on how we relate to one another more than it is our individual abilities. Indeed, even more so than a Super Bowl championship team, we thrive when there is focused vision; clear leadership; and strong, interconnected relationships.

WORKINGS OF MACHINES

Over the years, I've heard various motivational speakers exhort Christians to work together as parts of a machine, with command-and-control precision. That might be acceptable if the Bible called us a "robot of Christ" or a "machine of Christ," but it does not. Imagine how our lives would change if we resembled machine parts. Each person could focus solely on what he or she needed to do for the Christian machine to work. There would be no imperative to consider the plight of other, far-flung parts.

In our tightly controlled machine, we might interact only with other members in our immediate group. And we might miss any parts that malfunctioned or left. Bringing in new parts would have to be done carefully, because it might be a risky proposition to open up our group to outsiders. Each part of the machine would serve a narrow purpose. So, our calling and focus would be fairly obvious and unchanging. While the parts of the machine would undoubtedly have a few routines in a repetitive existence, the machine would offer the attractive quality of stability. People who fear the unknown could find comfort in this kind of secure environment.

Viewing ourselves as a body yields a much different scenario. Functioning like parts of a machine damages our intimacy with God and one another. For instance, when a man loses an arm, he compensates by using the other arm. A machine is less flexible. Losing a part (e.g., a car losing a tire) can incapacitate it. Somebody outside the machine maintains it. A machine is a tool created to perform work; it is a slave for the tasks its creator designed for it to carry out.

A living body adapts to its environment and responds purposefully, while a machine does not. A living organism gives glory to God simply by "being alive."

Humans build machines for the purpose of performing particular tasks. When we as Christians attempt to organize ourselves like a machine, though, we miss the main reason God created us and gave us life. We might be able to conduct church programs and events efficiently in a machinelike manner in the short term. But over the long term, we will miss the joy of life found in the body. I love this quote from philosophy professor Thomas Burke: "Because man has been created in God's image, his individual worth derives not from his utility in the world or even to God, but from his nature as a being in God's image. Because he is a free, responsible, rational person capable of true interpersonal communion with God and his fellow humans and of mirroring in those relationships and in his own mind and heart the very glory and goodness of the Lord, he can never be treated as a mere means to an end."[3] Burke understands the importance of the organic nature of human beings: we can never find true fulfillment and purpose as components of some sort of machine.

The distinction between living organisms and organizations runs deeper than a distinction from teams or machines. Members of a living body tend to sense ownership in that body. They reach fulfillment as the body becomes fulfilled, as if it were happening to them individually. As Paul said in his letter to the Romans: "Rejoice with those who rejoice; mourn with those who mourn" (Romans 12:15). This element of interconnectedness plays out in the business world, where enterprises thrive when they establish the sense (real or perceived) of employee ownership of the company.

DYNAMICS OF THE BODY

Why do polls consistently show that more than two-thirds of American workers are unhappy and not engaged in their jobs? Perhaps this stems from so many being treated like parts of a nonliving machine. After all, machine parts are owned by an entity outside of the machine and exist solely for the purposes of the owner of the machine. Such an organization's members tend to have a relationship with the whole that resembles an outside contractor instead of an owner.

One criticism of modern medical care is that caregivers have become like mechanics. It is easy to fall into the trap of treating a patient as if he or she is a physiological machine rather than a whole person—body, mind, and spirit. Driven by modern profit motives and management that values efficiency over relationship, medical science and the art of medicine often become degraded into a set of technical skills. This reduces doctors and nurses to medical technicians. But as a member of the medical profession, I can see that our patients long for caring interaction. They want doctors who will treat the whole person instead of quickly checking their chart and dispensing advice with the coldness of a computer-generated prescription.

A similar modern-day tragedy occurs in the church when we treat it like an organization. We must take care not to operate so rigidly that it becomes machinelike in its operations. People can't just be changed like a defective car muffler. Members of a body are interrelated in such a dynamic way that when one part is lost, it can never simply be replaced. All the other parts are affected by this loss and must, to some degree, change or adapt their roles. I can only imagine how new believers feel when a church treats them as a part of an organization rather than as vital members of a living body.

God took a big risk by choosing to make the Church a body rather than an organization. A living body is naturally unpredictable.

Apparently, God wants something other than slave-like machines. He wants a true relationship with us, even though that carries inherent risks. God has judged the risk to be worth it to allow the rich rewards of a relationship.

The Church is a body, with all the implications associated with that term. Being part of a body means vulnerability and intimacy with the other parts. This goes against my natural, Westernized inclination toward individuality and self-sufficiency. If I'm a member of a body, my sense of who I am must include people other than myself, including those I will never meet. That implies unusually close relationships among the members of the body around the world.

God must have a reason to use a term loaded with so much intimacy. To quote Professor Burke again:

> As staunch an individualist as Calvin holds that one comes into Christ only by way of that Church; the Christian has definite ethical obligations to his brothers and sisters in Christ; and the life eternal will take place in the context of a kingdom with a royal city, the new Jerusalem (Revelation 21:2). Man, in other words, is always part of a community of men and cannot re-move himself from the problems, cares, concerns, and aspirations of that community. This holds not only for his social existence, but especially for his religious life. While the individual can and ought to approach God as an individual, offering his own petitions and thanks-givings, he cannot rightly limit himself to such worship. Worship is a corporate endeavor, and the saints worship the Lord of Hosts as a unified body of synchronized worshippers. The Bible does not extol or encourage hermit Christians.[4]

God specifically uses the imagery of a living body to convey something essential about human relationships with one another: we are meant always to be in community, supporting, encouraging, and helping one another to function.

Core Characteristics

If the Church is a one-of-a-kind living creation of God, a living body, we must appreciate what that means if we are to fulfill our created purpose. The body of Christ doesn't prepare its own vision or set its own goals; they have already been arranged for us, recorded in the Bible. Our strength is not in our membership numbers or political know-how but in our interactions with one another and with the head of our body, Jesus Christ.

When we slide back into the top-down leadership configuration found in corporations, organizations, and government agencies, we lose our strongest witnesses to the world. They already know the worldly system of leadership. What they are in dire need of is for the body of Christ to exhibit the qualities found in living organisms—not to just imitate worldly organizations.

During Old Testament times, Israeli society came structured with a special class of priests at the pinnacle. Yet, in the New Testament church, the body of Christ requires every believer to be a minister before God. When we disregard this living structure that God designed, the rank-and-file believers, or "laity," surrender our God-given responsibility to minister. We aren't to have artificial church organizations that place professional super-Christians or "clergy" in charge of all ministry tasks. The ministers are to arise from the pews.

When we choose to continue the long-established traditions of church organizations, we find that our duties as believers are reduced to attending church services and listening to the pastor. Our evangelistic efforts are reduced to bringing the lost into the building so that they too can listen (a paradigm that is doomed in a modern world that spends more time on smartphones and interactive YouTube programming than passive TV viewing). Pastors tend to become victims of "burn out" in this scenario, while the church becomes weaker and less effective in reaching the world. This is often how we do things, though, if for no other reason than it's just the way we've always done them.

These habits have serious consequences. More than at any other time in years, today's Church influences the world less and is influenced by worldly culture more. The church in general has no weight of authority in the marketplace of ideas. The Church has had no nation-shaking revival during my six decades on this earth. This crying need for increased effectiveness is a good indication that we must change our way of thinking. We must leave behind the pragmatic, worldly approach to church organization and adopt a "living body" viewpoint. The solution is not to fine-tune our existing organizations. To fulfill our calling and destiny, we must trade nonliving organizational models for a living body. Our problem is not a lack of cleverness or lack of effort; it's an inaccurate view of who we are.

The way the modern church operates is a far cry from the idea that each individual believer is a minister, a vital player in the Church's outreach to the world. Each member of the body has gifts from the Holy Spirit, which means the entire body is to do the work of the ministry. I am grateful that pastors minister to our congregations, but the overarching need today is for congregations that will minister to the world. There must be a place for Jesus in your daily relationships and employment. This is the only way we can do "greater things" than Jesus did while on the earth and fulfill the promise He made in John 14:12.

COLLECTIVE BEHAVIOR

When groups of animals (e.g., colonies of ants, flocks of birds, schools of fish, or swarms of bees) get together, patterns emerge from the group as a whole. It may seem that a centralized controller is calling the shots, as if some magical Wizard of Oz is pulling levers behind the curtain. However, this is not the case. The group's behavior bubbles up from the individual members. They think locally and act locally, but when the actions of all the members are combined, it results in the group's broad behavior.

Look at an ant colony. While individual ants have little (if any) perception of the colony as a whole, their separate behaviors cause the colony to behave as one body. Ant colonies live about fifteen years, even though each ant lives only a few months. There is a continual turnover. How do the colonies progress and adapt over time without centralized control? This occurs because the colony's overall behavior arises from the combined behavior of all the ants, instead of from a central authority.

The majority of us don't take time to study the details of ants; we just want them to not annoy us. If we do take notice, it appears that the queen ant is the one in charge of the workers. Closer inspection reveals this isn't true. The queen ant doesn't control the colony. She functions only to produce baby ants. The same is true of the queen bee in a hive. In a remarkably similar manner, the actions of individual bees combine to form the behavior of a swarm. Despite the lack of centralized control, the group appears to act purposefully, as if it is a single being.

And so it is in the body of Christ. All of us have a free will to do as we see fit, and the overall behavior of the body emerges from our combined actions. Sometimes people in the church want to take over and control others, an impulse that may originate from noble intentions. But when this happens, it leads us away from being a living body in which the spirit of Christ is present as we gather together in His name.

Of course, this human desire for control isn't restricted to church management. It tends to promote top-down economies and business models. A living body does not thrive on top-down management, though. The behavior of the overall body "bubbles up" from individual cells and their interactions with their neighbor cells and surroundings. The communication among cells goes both ways. You influence your neighbor, and your neighbor influences you. All living systems have communication feedback loops.

Cells in a body each develop along different lines. To do this, they use more than just their copies of the genetic code. They develop a unique place and function in the body through their interactions with other cells. They learn from their neighbors. Amazingly, each of our cells has the tools needed for detecting neighbor cells, identifying which kind of cells they are, and communicating with them by means of chemical messengers.

ADAPTING TO SURROUNDINGS

This ingenious mode of operation means living bodies are able to adapt to their changing surroundings in ways unthinkable for a command-and-control arrangement. They contain diverse members that act locally and in right relationship with others so that the overall body remains healthy and functioning. In other areas of human activity, including business, the living-body model has proven much more resilient in turbulent times than has the outdated command-and-control management style. The study of living bodies now provides the foundation for avant-garde business theories.

Consider, for example, this observation from Paul Saffo, director of the Institute for the Future, in the book *The Biology of Business: Decoding the Natural Laws of Enterprise* (published 1999): "A funny thing happened to business in the last two decades—it turned upside down. Suddenly, the old rules no longer applied—stability became a liability, size an inconvenience, and command-and-control hierarchies an albatross. Business as usual became business as unusual: unpredictable, unplannable, and above all, unmanageable. Old giants tottered and new players burst into new markets, only to become roadkill for the next wave of upstarts."[5]

Basic biological principles can be applied in the business world to revolutionize its organizational structures and behavior. In business as in living systems, it is true that no manager can remain successful through forcing control. The desired results develop at the grassroots level by creating the right conditions and incentives for them to emerge. This is fundamentally different from traditional approaches that promote a strong central authority.

This authority focus is an inherent feature of organizations that, by their nature, must be organized. Men create them to accomplish particular tasks. Living bodies are organized too, but God created their organizational structure to give life. This is why we must avoid replacing the living body with institutionalized religion. This seems to represent a constant temptation for believers seeking certainty instead of a vibrant, ever-changing relationship with Christ. Rather than faith, we want something concrete around which to wrap our minds.

This craving for stability is a primary reason why the traditional local church model resembles a business organization that casts people into two molds: the ministers and the congregation. In this model, the senior pastor functions as the CEO, while other pastors and lay ministers are added to the staff as needed. As the experts, clergy members are at the top of the organizational chart and are the primary performers on stage. The congregation acts more like spectators than participants. The success of the performance can be measured by the size of the audience and the amount of money collected. It is little wonder that the meaning of body ministry gets lost.

Jesus sees things differently. In His ministry on Earth, He taught using examples and parables that borrowed from life. He spoke of plants growing in the fields, of faith like a mustard seed, and fishing for men. A trained carpenter, he could have spoken about building the House of God with metaphors that spoke of sanding, grinding, measuring, and as-sembling. Instead, Jesus used the living things around us as His teaching aids to describe the fingerprint of God on creation and how individuals should live in relationship to one another and to Him. People think in terms of organizations; God thinks in terms of organisms.

A living body functions from the bottom up. It sees only one kind of people: believers. Like an ant colony or a beehive, it sees the minis-try of Christ "bubbling up" from individual members and leadership arising naturally from within the membership ranks. Believers coalesce into functioning groups, often known as cell groups. Sunday morning services become more of a celebration or reunion of the body instead of the week's main ministry event.

In this model, the pastor doesn't try to play all the parts. He or she assumes the role of an encourager and equipper for the members/minis-ters. In this way, the local church provides a structure within which the unique gifts of the members can flourish. In *Unfinished Business*, Ogden observed, "In the New Testament the church is variously described as the household of God, the people of God, the bride of Christ, and a fellowship of the Holy Spirit. In fact, ninety-six word pictures of the church have been identified. Yet the image that permeates the New Testament understanding of the church and serves as an umbrella for all these metaphors is that of the church as the body of Christ."[6]

This is the body we need to see in action in today's ever more fractured, chaotic, and uncertain world. The way the laity in a traditional church structure becomes more involved is by becoming a part of the stage crew as ushers, lighting crew, sound crew, and background instruments to enhance the production—what some people label as "the Sunday morning show." As we become a living body, we promote religious performance less and the diffuse, unorchestrated ministry of all believers more. As members of the body, we can be most effective and genuine to the world the less our ministry is confined to a church building. An analogy from the medical world might be that it's better to have functioning kidneys always with you wherever you go than being restricted to a dialysis unit several times a week.

Only when the church functions as an organism instead of as an organization will we see it fulfill its mission and rise to the heights God created for His body to attain.

QUESTIONS FOR DISCUSSION

1. Why do you think God created the church to be a living body rather than a business or an organization? What difference does this make?
2. How are the relationships among members of a business or an organization different from relationships between members of a living body? Do you want to see the latter in your church? Why?
3. Like a machine, an organization is a tool created by man to perform work. How do you see this as different from a living body?
4. God created us for relationship with Him. How might it have been less risky if He had created the church to be an organization instead of a living body?

5. How does the strength of the body of Christ stem from our interactions with one another?

6. How can we be hindered by having an inaccurate view of who we are as believers?

7. If we become more like a living body, we promote "religious performance" less and the unorchestrated ministry of all believers more. How do you think this can help transform our relationships?

CHAPTER
5

KNIT TOGETHER

I am told that Christians do not love each other. I am very sorry if
that be true, but I rather doubt it, for I suspect that those who do
not love each other are not Christians.[1]

—**LEGENDARY BRITISH PREACHER CHARLES SPURGEON**

One day, as I assisted a surgeon, he had me reach into the patient's chest and turn his heart so he could work on it from a better angle. As I gingerly swiveled it, he asked, "How does it feel to hold a man's beating heart in your hand?" For a moment, I stood speechless, in awe of this organ beating beneath my own fluttering heart. The fact that it continued to function while I held it in my hand fascinated me. In spite of our manipulations, the man's heart kept thumping as billions of tiny heart cells communicated and coordinated their activities. It is much tougher to take the miracle of life for granted when you have watched its intricate details up close, aware that the least little malfunction could alter a person's life span.

The cells in your heart contract rhythmically in orchestral unity, acting together to produce a heartbeat. The contractions of the individual cells are synchronized so the heart can efficiently pump blood to your body. If these living cells are separated from the heart in a test tube, they will instinctively continue beating—but not in coordination with each other. I saw this firsthand during medical school while separating animal heart cells in a physiology lab. I watched through the microscope and slowly brought them in contact with one another, and the instant they touched, their contractions became synchronized.

That is the nature of heart cells. Individual heart cells cannot accomplish their God-given function and calling alone; they were designed to be one of many cells in one heart. While they serve a unique function in the body, they are not useful if they don't communicate and coordinate their efforts. Indeed, if the members of an entire body don't communicate, life is not possible. A single heart cell working alone cannot pump blood to the body, no matter how hard it tries. It needs the other cells to fulfill its purpose.

This is a consistent pattern found in all living bodies. The only way a body can survive is through its many members working together. This physical reality demonstrates that what happens in the body comes about by the interactions of the members with one another. All living bodies have communication among the members.

INTERNAL COMMUNICATION

Communication among members of the body is reciprocal. You influence your neighbor, and your neighbor influences you. Thus, God's plan: many members working together as one body. God didn't design any believers to become "super Christians" and triumph over the devil with solitary, supernatural skills. We need one another to accomplish Christ's ministry here on earth. When Jesus said we would "do even greater things than these" (John 14:12), I believe He was referring to us as members of the body of Christ, not calling us to be spectacular, miracle-working individuals able to do a better job than He did.

As an organ, the heart does an amazing job of circulating our blood every second of our lives, but it consists of many "member" cells. This is God's pattern for life. In the book of Genesis, as He created us in His image, God spoke of mankind in plural terms. Interestingly, He also used plural terms for Himself: "Then God said, 'Let *us* make man in *our* image, in *our* likeness, and let *them* rule over the fish of the sea and the birds of the air, over the livestock, over all the earth, and over all the creatures that move along the ground.' So God created man in his own image, in the image of God he created him; male and female he created *them*" (Genesis 1:26–27, emphasis added).

If the Bible uses plural terms for the triune God who created us in His image, then it should not be surprising that we are meant to function as many members blending into one cohesive unit.

During my years in various churches, I have often heard the phrase "membership matters," which is true of the body of Christ. Consequently, how can we discern who is a member of this body and who is not? The Bible provides some general guidelines:

- "If anyone acknowledges that Jesus is the Son of God, God lives in them and they in God" (1 John 4:15).
- "Not everyone who says to me, 'Lord, Lord,' will enter the kingdom of heaven, but only he who does the will of my Father who is in heaven" (Matthew 7:21).
- "Dear friends, let us love one another, for love comes from God. Everyone who loves has been born of God and knows God. Whoever does not love does not know God, because God is love" (1 John 4:7–8).

People who recognize the sovereignty of God, do His will, and love both Him and each other have the Bible-described marks of members of the body of Christ. Still, God alone ultimately determines who is or is not a member of the body. Jesus emphasized this truth in His parable about heaven in Matthew 13. The sower planted wheat seeds in his field, but an enemy came and planted weeds among them. When the wheat sprouted and formed heads, the weeds appeared. When his servants asked if he wanted them to pull them up, he answered: "No . . . because while you are pulling the weeds, you may uproot the wheat with them. Let both grow together until the harvest. At that time I will tell the harvesters: First collect the weeds and tie them in bundles to be burned; then gather the wheat and bring it into my barn" (Matthew 13:29–30).

BEACON OF HOPE

This parable reveals that it isn't up to us to decide whom to admit or exclude. It would be helpful if we could immediately ascertain the spiritual status of those we meet. However, it is difficult to know what resides inside a person's heart. It usually takes an extended amount of time, personal encounters, and close observation to draw an informed view. (Even then, we can't be 100 percent sure, according to Proverbs 21:2: "A person may think their own ways are right, but the LORD weighs the heart.") Maybe this is because God doesn't want us to draw lines too quickly, defining who's in and who's out of the body.

Think about this physical illustration. If my hand strikes my knee, my knee isn't aware of whether or not the hand striking it is part of its body. It just knows it was struck. The knee doesn't need to be concerned with figuring out the particulars; it only has to obey the head. The head knows what is part of the body and what isn't and directs the members' activities. The members just have to obey the head and not get side-tracked by other issues. When we recognize we are part of the body of Christ, we will live our lives less as individuals and more as members of the one body.

The Church consists of imperfect people, each with limitations, shortcomings, and flaws. During the last two thousand years, the Church in general and individual believers in particular have fallen short of perfection. Despite these errors, no other force in history has been a brighter beacon of hope in the midst of darkness.

Take, for example, the scholarly research that sociologist Robert Woodberry conducted, which he initiated during his doctoral studies at the University of North Carolina. He set out to determine why some nations develop stable, representative democracies where people enjoy the rights to vote, speak, and assemble freely while other, neighboring countries suffer under dictatorial rule, internal dissension, and inferior health and economic growth. Thanks to extensive studies and worldwide travels, Woodberry came up with an answer. Where missionaries were free in the nineteenth and twentieth centuries to establish systems of schools, printed materials, and other advancements, societies developed into more democratic, prosperous nations.

Woodberry developed historical proof that missionaries had educated women and the poor; promoted widespread printing; led nationalist movements that empowered ordinary people; and fueled other key elements of democracy. He learned that statistics backed up the reality that missionaries weren't just part of the picture, but central to it—findings he subjected to peer-reviewed studies and sometimes-skeptical academic audiences.

"I was shocked," Woodberry told journalist Andrea Palpant Dilley, who chronicled his discoveries in *Christianity Today*. "It was like an atomic bomb. The impact of missions on global democracy was *huge*. I kept adding variables to the model—factors that people had been studying and writing about for the past 40 years—and they all got wiped out. It was amazing. I knew then that I was on to something really important. The results were so strong, they made me nervous. I expected an effect, but I had not expected it to be that large or powerful. I thought, *I better make sure this is real. I better be very careful.*"[2]

The research held up, according to Daniel Philpott, who teaches political science at the University of Notre Dame. Philpott told Dilley, "For [Woodberry] to show through devastatingly thorough analysis that conversionary Protestants are crucial to what makes the country democratic today [is] remarkable in many ways. Not only is it another factor—it turns out to be the most important factor. It can't be anything but startling for scholars of democracy."[3]

MAKING AN IMPACT

Christians coming together to serve others makes a powerful impact on societies. One reason is—unlike government programs that maintain a decidedly secular flavor—they are free to address underlying spiritual problems. Take Teen Challenge, the faith-based program founded by the late David Wilkerson, author of the legendary bestseller *The Cross and the Switchblade*. Launched in the late 1950s, it established its first residential center several years later and now operates nearly two hundred residential centers nationwide.

Throughout its history, this ministry has shown remarkable success. Of a sample of 1,968 graduates in its flagship Pennsylvania program, 95 percent of graduates were abstaining from the use of heroin seven years after graduation, and 87.5 percent of them were abstaining from the use of marijuana. In 1994, a study at the University of Tennessee found that 86 percent of Teen Challenge graduates were abstaining from drugs.[4]

The most recent study by Wilder Research of 315 men, women, and youth—who graduated from a yearlong life care program in Minnesota—showed impressive results as well. The survey tracked graduates from 2007 to 2009 and determined that 74 percent of adult program graduates reported no drug use for the previous six months. Sixty-two percent reported no relapses since graduation or use in the previous six months. Seventy-seven percent were working at least thirty hours a week or were full-time students; 58 percent had attended school since graduating from Teen Challenge. Eighty percent rated the program's overall quality as "outstanding" or "very good." When asked to identify what helped the most, graduates mentioned the program's faith-based aspects most often.[5]

Former White House aide and convicted Watergate conspirator Charles Colson saw similar results when he founded Prison Fellowship as a faith-based program aimed at helping reform the lives of inmates. He saw too many going through a revolving door of prison, reoffending, and returning to lock-up. Forty years later, Colson is no longer alive, but this ministry remains healthy. It maintains a presence in more than fourteen hundred prisons in all fifty states, reaching some two hundred thousand inmates. In addition to partnerships with eight thousand churches, it engages some seventy-four hundred volunteers across the United States.

What's more, studies have shown that faith-based programming helps reduce recidivism—the revolving door that affects far too many prisoners; the national average is 43 percent. It is more than 60 percent in Minnesota, the state where Prison Fellowship introduced its InnerChange initiative in 2002, five years after it started the program in Texas. Minnesota's Department of Corrections later conducted a study of the thirty-month program, which attempts to help participants transition from prison to the community through educational, faith-based programming—including mentorship. The state found that participation in InnerChange significantly decreased the risk of reoffending, including rearrest (26 percent), reconviction (35 percent), and new offense reincarceration (40 percent).[6]

BENEFITS OF BENEVOLENCE

I have seen the value of Christian compassion firsthand. For more than thirty years, my parents have operated benevolence programs for the unbelievably poor people of Haiti, working with churches there to provide schools, housing, feeding programs, and medical clinics. The people live in squalor, with many housed in mud huts or lean-tos fashioned from tree limbs, leaves, and cardboard. Many often go without food for days at a time. Medical care is typically nonexistent. When these people receive government handouts, they can continue to subsist for a while, but their lives do not change significantly. Their dysfunctional patterns of behavior continue, as do their fractured relationships with other people and God. The help they receive is superficial and temporary. However, when Christian ministries provide the gospel message along with material relief, the people find hope. Numerous lives are changed in a vital way. We have seen entire villages transformed.

While many consider Haitians as impoverished and ignorant, the way of addressing social problems in the United States is frequently just as abysmal. Treating needy people without addressing their underlying spiritual problems draws the life out of the caregivers. In government clinics for the poor, those with self-defeating personal behaviors often return repeatedly for treatment. They may experience relationship problems with their families, which go unaddressed. Those who have no relationship with God usually continue in self-destructive lifestyles. Yet because prayer is prohibited in such settings and the Bible or God cannot be discussed, the problems persist. Providers cannot label dysfunctional behavior as destructive—that would be "discriminatory."

Thus, these patients often continue such behavior until the consequences of their actions make them sick. Then they come back for treatment so they can resume their self-destructive behavior. For those providing the care, it can seem like a vicious cycle with no end in sight. Trying to change unwanted behavior without modifying underlying spiritual problems is like putting a bandage on a cancer. We need to be wise enough to look at the underlying eternal issues and not just what's immediately obvious.

A Positive Impact

I have seen the positive impact that Christian-based medical ministry can make in this country. Treating people in settings where both prayer and medicine are provided and spiritual issues are addressed is like a breath of fresh air. I've seen nurses gladly volunteer in these settings when they would never consider working at secular or government-operated clinics.

One example is a clinic for the poor I started while serving as the codirector of a trauma center at a university medical center. We saw about forty thousand emergency patients annually and another sixty thousand patients at an adjoining ambulatory care clinic. At both sites, a seemingly endless stream of needy patients came off the streets. While we gave them the best care we could for their bodies, we couldn't address their spiritual needs due to various limitations.

Feeling the urge to do more, I took my little black bag and a stethoscope to bridges and other places where the homeless congregated. I typically made these "house calls" on Saturday nights and early Sunday mornings. These contacts opened doors for relationships, prayers, and invitations to church. Through these visits, I got to know the leaders of a rescue mission; they offered the use of their cafeteria early Sunday mornings for an indoor clinic. Not only was this a step up for my informal treatments, but people at my church also became involved. A businessman provided free use of a building in the inner city to see patients during the week. Area hospitals donated medical equipment and supplies from their warehouses, and nurses and other helpers volunteered their time.

We ended up with a full-time free medical clinic, where prayer partners were paired with each patient. They accompanied them through the process to develop a relationship, learn more about their personal needs, and discern their spiritual condition. We prayed with every patient and even had a designated prayer room where we could conduct extended prayer sessions and counseling. People came to Christ and received healing and deliverance from personal problems. I networked with more than fifty area pastors, who agreed to pray for patients and continue counseling and other services after they left the clinic.

One of the most encouraging developments in all this was the attitude of the nurses and other medical workers. They loved volunteering there, which wasn't surprising because so many in medicine go into the field with a sincere desire to help people. However, in their paid positions, they ran a daily gauntlet for completing everyday tasks, including satisfying the expectations of third-party payers, hospital administrators, government regulators, and attorneys. It is not unusual to lose heart and experience burnout amid such pressures, especially in a secular environment where attempting to address spiritual needs brings immediate reprisals and possible legal action.

Our society desperately needs faith-based initiatives like that clinic, along with more church members who are willing to venture outside of their church to see how the rest of the world lives. After all, it is hard to scan any website or social-media portal today without sensing the hopelessness and despair that exist in people's lives. While we are without a doubt the most prosperous generation in recorded history, we often sense that the world is collapsing around us. People face a steady stream of anguish and hopelessness. Terrorist attacks, pandemics, grisly crimes, racial strife, and natural disasters happen. Many people sense they are in desperate need of *something*; they just don't know what they desperately need.

This is when the need for a unified body of Christ is clear. Those in the New Testament accounts did not *go to* church. They *were* the Church. Ministry in the church should be thought of as an occurrence rather than as an authorized position. Christ's body serves the purpose of allowing Him to interact with this physical world. So, the concept of this divine body is especially pertinent today. A key issue has to do with finding out who we are as Christians and what role we play in the grand scheme of things. Are we passive, complacent, and disjointed? Will we come together to become effective salt and light in this world? Will we experience revival (with revival beginning first in our hearts)?

THE HEAD

Identifying solutions to the crying needs of today's world doesn't rely on human intelligence, reasoning, or political machinations. We can know what we are to do by relying on the Holy Spirit to convey the will, mind, and heart of the Father. We have written directions in the Bible as well. Paul's letter to the Ephesians spells out how Christ gave His church apostles, prophets, evangelists, pastors, and teachers to equip His followers for works of service and to build up the body so we could attain unity, knowledge of the Son of God, and spiritual maturity. The result is that we won't be like infants who are tossed around by waves and winds of false doctrines taught by deceptive and deceitful leaders. Paul concludes his teaching by saying that, "Instead, speaking the truth in love, we will grow to become in every respect the mature body of him who is the head, that is, Christ. From him the whole body, joined and held together by every supporting ligament, grows and builds itself up in love, as each part does its work" (Ephesians 4:15–16).

Because you and I are not the head of the church, we should be slow to order others to do what we have been called to do. We are merely members and, as such, take orders from Christ as the head. If others are called to join us in our calling, that is great. But it should be the head and not us who calls them to the task. This connection is vital, as shown by Paul's warning to the Colossians to not allow others to judge them because of what they ate or drank or whether they followed certain religious festivals and Sabbath observances and not to be deceived by those who delighted in false humility and worship of angels. The apostle said of those who get puffed up with the idle notions of an unspiritual mind, "They have lost connection with the head, from whom the whole body, supported and held together by its ligaments and sinews, grows as God causes it to grow" (Colossians 2:19).

The body of Christ and all its parts are necessary for our growth and functioning. The human body is a perfect parallel. If you pick up an apple, you don't extend yourself through the hand to pick it up; the hand is part of you. Likewise, we are the body of Christ. Perhaps we aren't so much an extension of Christ here on earth as much as we *are* Christ's body for the world. This point of view takes our will out of the picture and emphasizes the priority of doing the will of God.

THE BONE CONNECTION

Much as our bones serve as anchors for other parts of our body to function normally, the body of Christ is organized around supportive structures. Again, the parallels to the human body are remarkable. For instance, consider the Greek word *orthos*, which means "correct," "straight," or "upright." From this root comes the medical specialty known as ortho-pedics, a discipline that treats bone problems so a body can be correct, straight, or upright. In our spiritual lives, orthodoxy is a theological term referring to correct, straight, or upright beliefs.

Each of us has bones that together form a skeleton, which supports other parts of our body and provides a foundation for them to function. Think of what our bodies would be like without bones. Maybe we could contract our muscles, but there would be nothing solid for them to pull against. We would not be able to stand upright, walk, or even lift our arms. This is because effective movement isn't possible without adequate structural framework. The soft or fluid parts of the body can function well only when paired up with the solid parts.

Our bones are made by cells (called osteoblasts) at specific areas along the bones (termed ossification centers). At birth, we have few hardened bones in our bodies; most are pliable. As we mature into adulthood, our bones start to harden. When we reach old age, our bones can eventually become brittle and are easily broken. This is a picture of how each member plays a structural role in the body of Christ. It seems that our development can mirror the development of bones in our physical bodies. When we first become Christians, we may possess a good deal of flexibility. We are open to new ways of doing things, eager to see the Holy Spirit move, and eager for God to change lives. However, over time, we can become set in our ways. We can easily equate cultural or church traditions with Scripture and old habits with biblical thinking. As believers, we can become as calcified as old, brittle bones.

Don't misunderstand. I'm not dismissing elderly members as unimportant, hidebound traditionalists. Bones in our physical bodies serve an anchoring function. Backbones provide a foundation for the functions of other parts. But hardening does not always serve the body well. For instance, a kidney stone may harden and form a blockage to the natural flow, causing significant pain and disability. In the same way, well-intentioned people may feel compelled to prevent natural growth and development in the local church. They may think that by preventing change they are avoiding chaos and disaster or keeping deceptive troublemakers from sowing dissension in the congregation.

How can we determine whether, by standing firm, we are functioning as a healthy piece of the foundation or as an unhealthy blockage? One way to discern this is to ask how we view change. Are we yearning to return to the "good old days"? Or do we have a clear vision for what we are to become in Christ? Are we looking forward or backward? Are we so dissatisfied with the way things are that we are willing to follow a difficult—even painful—course to improve them? Or is our energy primarily focused on maintaining what has been done previously and seeking the most comfortable path so we can continue chasing the "American Dream" of living life in the pursuit of personal peace and affluence?

While we appreciate the structural components, or "bones," in the body of Christ, it's important to maintain balance between the rigid and the flowing—for instance, the balance between truth and mercy. If the solid components do not work in concert with the softer, fluid parts, then our ability to minister suffers.

My wife, Lydia, had a negative experience that might serve as an example. As part of her Bible school training, she was assigned to work alongside fellow students as they preached on the streets of Dallas. She recalls, "Their approach was to yell at passersby about being sinners and burning in hell. I remember the angry looks on the faces of people as they crossed the street to try to avoid us. I actually separated myself from the team, found people who looked as if they needed a friend, began to witness one on one to them, and actually was able to lead a number of people to the Lord that way because they saw I cared about them as a person.

"They knew it was probably true they were going to hell, but truth alone couldn't reach them. It was the balance of truth and mercy. In fact, I remember the people I talked to saying they knew they were in sin. They already knew the truth. They wanted someone to care about them and love them and respond to them with love—not with the rod of truth alone. I don't consider nonbelievers as objects to evangelize but as people who deserve all the love and consideration we can give them because they were made in the image of God."

My wife's ability to flexibly and compassionately respond to the needs of the people she was witnessing to instead of rigidly chastising them enabled her to reach others in a way her companions in her evangelism could not. The "soft" parts of the body serve their own purpose.

QUESTIONS FOR DISCUSSION

1. Individual heart cells need others to serve their purpose in the body. How do members in the body of Christ need one another to be effective?
2. In Genesis 1, God refers to Himself in plural terms, yet He is one God. What do you think that means for us as human beings, created in His image?
3. Read 1 John 4:15, Matthew 7:21, and 1 John 4:7-8. Then answer the question: Although God alone decides who is or is not a member of the body of Christ, what can help us discern this in everyday life?
4. Although the Church consists of imperfect people, no force in history has been a brighter beacon of hope in the midst of darkness. Why do you think this is so?

5. Trying to change unwanted behavior without altering underlying spiritual problems can be futile. How should this influence our benevolence programs?

6. What is the difference between going to church and being the Church?

7. As we interact with others, how do you think we can best maintain a balance between truth and mercy?

CHAPTER
6

THE ESSENCE OF LIFE

The thief comes only to steal and kill and destroy;
I have come that they may have life, and have it to the full.

—JESUS IN JOHN 10:10

One prolife group estimates that more than fifty-seven million abortions were performed in the forty years after the Supreme Court handed down its *Roe v. Wade* ruling.[1] This 1973 decision effectively legalized abortion on demand. While the sheer numbers are overwhelming, I remember one in particular. This baby accomplished the impossible—surviving the abortionist's attempt to snuff out his life. Though strong enough to temporarily live outside the womb, he was too young to survive for very long after being separated from his mother, primarily because his lungs weren't developed adequately enough to support his body's needs. Medical science had failed to kill him quickly, and now medical science had little to offer that would allow him to live. The nurses called me to the operating room where his abortion was in progress.

At the time, I had been a physician for about three years. I had seen a few aborted fetuses who still had a heartbeat. But this infant wasn't lying limp like the others were doing. He was moving his arms and legs and looked as if he wanted to cry—a rather embarrassing situation for the abortionist. The situation struck me as absurd. Just minutes earlier, this fragile human being had legally been a "nonperson" possessing no rights. Yet, after surviving the abortion, he had magically become a "person" entitled to medical care (however inadequate that care happened to be).

The same system that had failed to kill him was now in charge of saving his life.

I transferred him to the neonatal intensive care unit (NICU) when it became obvious to me that this infant was too tough to die quickly. Attendants placed him under a heating lamp for warmth in his NICU baby bed. As I stared down at his frail body, emotion arose in my chest with each tiny heartbeat. I had the impression that the entire universe revolved around this one human being. I had often written routine orders for premature babies' admittance to the NICU, but this admission clearly was not routine.

Over several hours, as his breathing became more labored, he grimaced several times—evidence of a struggle with something he had no ability to comprehend. While I could see him, with his eyes fused shut he could not see me. He would never know me or remember me, but I would always remember him. Finally, his grunting quieted, his movements ceased, and the grimace passed. Though he was no longer breathing, his heartbeat continued. (It isn't unusual for babies' hearts to keep beating for some time after they are in all other ways dead.) Because of the irreversible brain damage he had sustained due to lack of oxygen, I pronounced him dead.

I've tried to understand why so many babies like this little boy can be killed while others of us have our lives and rights protected. I have posed that question to medical peers who perform abortions and have been surprised by the numbers who justify them based on economics. A typical response: "It's cheaper in the long run for taxpayers to pay for abortions rather than letting unwanted babies be born and become a burden to society." (The majority of patients at the county hospital where I worked then were poor, and tax money paid for most of their medical care.)

Our government allows for nonviolent change in law. When we the people judge a law to be immoral, we can modify it through elected officials. The time is ripe for additional laws against abortion. In the same way various states have moved to restrict unfettered access to this heartless practice in recent years, reasonable people should act to prevent more unborn babies from being categorized as "nonpersons" and extinguished before they can draw one breath. Whether or not abortion is wrong is not the question on which we should focus. The question is whether we will effect change in our world. Will our children someday hang their heads in shame because of what we allowed to be done to their brothers and sisters? Abortion is a sin against those among us who are the most innocent and vulnerable.

What Is Life?

This experience early in my medical career profoundly influenced my outlook on abortion and life in general. What is life? For several millennia, people have pondered that question. Until the last few centuries, societies typically had a poorly developed understanding of our existence. Some thought a physical substance causes objects to be alive. Life residing in the blood is an example of this physical theory. We now know that nothing physical gives life to any animal or human. Scientists and doctors have established that the condition of being alive occurs when a set of attributes is present. Life is a condition that can be observed over time rather than a thing that can be touched and handled.

Most people have an instinctive, basic understanding of the qualities of life; there are various ways to organize and study them. I will review the qualities of life as defined by science. Scientists know an organism is alive when it exhibits certain attributes that are necessary for an organism to live. A nonliving thing may have some or even most of these characteristics, but only those that possess all of them are considered to be alive. Things that don't are dead.

Occasionally, questions arise over whether or not a thing is truly alive. I remember students back in my high school biology class discussing whether or not viruses should be considered living things. After all, viruses are hijackers and must take over the machinery of a living cell to reproduce. Since they can't reproduce on their own, viruses don't exhibit all the processes found in living things. While some differences of opinion exist in various areas of science and biology, the emerging consensus over the years is that viruses are not living organisms.

Years later, the question my high school class discussed still intrigues me. I now see similar attributes in all the living things God made. This should be anticipated and can help us uncover what we would expect of the body of Christ if it were alive. It was eye opening to me when I realized the body of Christ meets the scientific conditions for being alive—that is, when it is functioning as described in the Bible. When we consider the attributes of living things, we can see how these traits are woven into the patterns of life found in the body of Christ. Because it has these qualities, it fits the definition of "living organism."

As the continuing debates over abortion demonstrate, it is surprisingly difficult to reach a consensus about what life is and when it begins. Life cannot be defined by what the thing is made of, since there aren't physical substances that make something alive. For instance, a recently deceased body has all the substances and complexity of a living body, but it is as lifeless as a rock. In the book of Ezekiel, the Lord takes the prophet Ezekiel out to a valley of dry bones from which all the life had departed (Ezekiel 37:1–15). The bones had been exposed to the elements to the point that they were becoming one with the elements; they had once been alive, but the life was gone. The Lord speaks to the bones and grants them new life; his power brings them back from the dead.

Life is not a substance; it is a condition that exists through the grace and power of God. We can see the fingerprint of God in the signature he writes on all living organisms he has created, the attributes of life that they all have in common.

MOVEMENT

In chapter 3, we discussed how movement is one of the first and most important indicators of a living organism. Many human beings seek orderly, calm stability. Movement and change can be unsettling for any group, including churches. Yet it is only when they are dead that living things are finally stable. A grim truism in the ER is that patients are entirely stable and unchanging only after they are dead.

Movement is a vital signifier of the fingerprint of God on all living things He has created. It expresses an aspect of His nature. *All living things move.* This movement may not be visible to the unaided eye, but nevertheless, it is always present. It may be movement detectable only with the aid of a microscope or unseen deep inside the organism, yet it is still movement.

This motion inside a living organism tends to have a "give and take" quality. Blood circulates. Every part of the body has blood entering it, but this means that blood is also going back out through circulation. There exists both an "intake" and an "output" of blood, which means we cannot hoard blood in one part of our body and survive. Another instance of this give-and-take, circular quality of movement is breathing. You can't just take in air; you need to exhale too. If you try to hold your breath too long, you may suffocate and die. This is additionally true in the spiritual realm. God gives us much as members of the body of Christ, but we must give it away to live and grow.

Life flows and changes with time. A living body adapts to its environment. Each member of a living body is able to change its position and tasks when required to do so for the overall good. These changes come about according to the season, time, or demands placed on the body from the outside. This is part of its dynamic nature. This is why the body of Christ must function as a living body, not as a stale organization. The world is the environment in which the body of Christ lives and moves. The body is called upon to perform different functions in its environment at different times. Thus, the individual members are required to serve with their various gifts and abilities, depending on the situation at hand.

We live in a world that is constantly changing. The body of Christ must change methods—not the message—to remain healthy in this shifting environment. We need to be a dynamic, adaptable body, yet one that remains true to its purpose even though individual members come and go over time. This is a quality of living bodies. Individual cells that constitute our bodies are replaced over and over again.

WAVES IN A STREAM

To better grasp what I mean, picture a shallow, fast-moving stream with a wave formed by a rock lying just under the surface. My two sons and I saw this on a whitewater rafting trip through the Grand Canyon a few summers ago. During our six-day journey down the Colorado River, we encountered numerous named rapids. The most memorable: Sockdolager Rapid, which we were told is translated "knockout blow." It is well named!

Individual water droplets that make up a wave constantly move as the river flows; nevertheless, the wave retains its qualities, such as location, shape, and size. We may think of things that are constant as being static. But as in the example of the wave, constancy is made possible only through the constant flow and replacement of individual drops of water.

Constancy in a living body is made possible through the continuous replacement of the cells. For instance, your body today has almost none of the same cells of which you were composed last year. And yet, you remain you. So, the person known as "you" is independent of your component parts. Who you are cannot be determined by examining each of your cells individually. Who you are emerges from the interactions among the cells in your body over time.

The body of Christ continues to exist even though there is a constant turnover of its membership. And the nature of this body is established not by the gifts and abilities of individual believers but by the interactions among its members over time. The Spirit of Christ arises "in our midst" as we live in right relationship with one another. Since the spirit of Christ arises through the interactions among the members, it cannot be fully appreciated from merely examining the members as individuals. The relevant Scripture comes from Matthew 18:20: "For where two or three are gathered together in My name, I am there in the midst of them" (NKJV). Although Christ may be in us individually, He did not emphasize, "There I am in each of them." He said He's "in the midst" of the gathering. Between us. The Spirit of Christ arises from the interactions of believers who are in right relationship with one another.

Think again about the human body. It is estimated that our bodies contain about seventy-five trillion cells. These cells are of different types but make up one body. In a sense, as an individual you are the summation of the behavior of all these individual cells. Without them you are nothing, but with them you are you. Several hundred cells die and are replaced every minute of your life. This means you now have billions of cells incorporated into your body that were not there last week. Just as the ants in a colony or the bees in a hive are continuously dying and being replaced, the cells in your body are in constant flux.

Because it is a living entity, the body of Christ also has constant flux among its members, but the body of Christ continues its life in spite of its constantly changing personnel.

A CREATOR IN COMMON

At one time, I thought similarities between the human body and the body of Christ meant they only mirrored each other. But now I appreciate a deeper lesson. The similarities between the human body and the body of Christ exist because they were both created by God. They appear to have similarities because each shows the nature, or "fingerprint," of God.

For those of you who enjoy math, it might look like this:

Without the Creator considered: A=B and B=A
Characteristics of the human body are reflected on the body of Christ. And characteristics of the body of Christ are reflected on the human body.

With the Creator considered: A=C and B=C; therefore, A=B
Characteristics of the Creator are reflected on the human body. And characteristics of the Creator are reflected on the body of Christ. As a result, there are similarities between the human body and the body of Christ.

It's not that the human body is patterned after the body of Christ or, conversely, that the body of Christ is patterned after the human body. Both reflect a third aspect, the nature of God. That's why they are similar. Evolutionists point to similarities among different species as proof of evolution. But it is more likely this proves that different species have the same creator rather than the same ancestors.

Parables that Jesus told explained spiritual truths by using everyday events. These parables are enlightening because the spiritual realm and the physical world have similarities, which exist because they have a creator in common. Matthew, the former tax collector who recorded the first of the four Gospels, noted that Christ always relied on stories with a parallel lesson or deeper meaning: "Jesus spoke all these things to the crowd in parables; he did not say anything to them without using a parable. So was fulfilled what was spoken through the prophet: 'I will open my mouth in parables, I will utter things hidden since the creation of the world'" (Matthew 13:34–35).

Jesus told stories simple enough for everyone to understand, including the common people of His day. The illustrations He used were visible, physical objects from everyday life, but they taught valuable spiritual lessons. His parables were clear and effective because the fingerprint of God is on all things He creates, whether seen or unseen. We can visualize and understand the spiritual world we can't see if we study the characteristics held in common with physical objects we can see.

In the Gospels, Jesus used parables to compare people to wheat or branches, the kingdom of God to a mustard seed or a tree, and the Word of God to seed. Later, in the epistles, the writers utilized the human body as a picture to describe the body of Christ.

Consider, for example, the story of Jesus and the coin related in Matthew 22, in which the Pharisees tried to set a verbal trap for the Lord by sending their disciples to pose a seemingly pious question. After praising His integrity, His teaching of the way of God in accordance with the truth, and His refusal to be swayed by others' views or social standing, they wanted to know whether it was proper to pay the imperial taxes demanded by Rome.

Their phony pretense didn't fool Jesus, who first asked why these hypocrites were trying to trap Him. Then He said: "'Show me the coin used for paying the tax.' They brought him a denarius, and he asked them, 'Whose image is this? And whose inscription?' 'Caesar's,' they replied. Then he said to them, 'So give back to Caesar what is Caesar's, and to God what is God's'" (Matthew 22:19–21).

Since the coin had Caesar's name and picture on it, Jesus instructed them to give it back to the rightful owner. In a similar way, we are created in the image of God and are to offer ourselves back to Him as a living sacrifice. Paul reinforced this idea in his letter to the Romans: "Therefore, I urge you, brothers and sisters, in view of God's mercy, to offer your bodies as a living sacrifice, holy and pleasing to God—this is your true and proper worship" (Romans 12:1).

THE IMPORTANCE OF SYMBOLS

As a young father, I once attempted to sketch a horse for my daughter. Although I told her it was a horse, later—as we drove through the countryside—she saw animals in the fields. While she called them horses, most were, in fact, cows. I had given her an idea about what a horse is but had not explained what it is not.

Symbolism plays an important role in learning. It allows us to comprehend attributes of a lesser-known object by comparing and contrasting it with something well known. This is why Paul used familiar objects during his discussion with nonbelievers on Mars Hill. He used the familiar idols they worshipped to introduce God to them by noting their altar TO AN UNKNOWN GOD. "You are ignorant of the very thing you worship," Paul told them, "and this is what I am going to proclaim to you" (Acts 17:23).

If you and I tried to strike up a conversation about AN UNKNOWN GOD with someone today, that person would consider us mad. It is not an operative concept in the minds of most modern people. It was on the minds of people that day on Mars Hill, though, so Paul used what they were familiar with to describe the unseen spiritual realm with which they were not familiar.

That is what I love about the term "body of Christ." It uses something physical with which we are all familiar to teach us rich lessons about things we cannot see.

Questions for Discussion

1. How the cells (or members) of a body interact determines life and death. If the body of Christ is alive, what does this mean for us as believers?

2. The processes of a living body often involve "give and take" as we breathe in and breathe out or as blood is pumped from the heart to the body and then back again. What application can you see to the body of Christ?

3. This chapter noted that movement and change sometimes unsettle and unnerve people as well as churches. How do you feel about the rapid pace of change in today's society?

4. In this chapter's example of the wave in a fast-moving stream, the shape of the wave endures, but only through the continuous turnover of water droplets over time. How does the body of Christ remain consistent in spite of ever-changing membership?

5. The human body is not patterned after the body of Christ. And the body of Christ is not patterned after the human body. So why do you think there are there similarities between the two?

6. The physical world and the spiritual realm have the same creator. How does this make parables an effective way to explain the spiritual realm?

CHAPTER 7

GOD MEETS ALL OUR NEEDS

And the Church must be forever building,
And always decaying,
And always being restored.[1]
—T. S. ELIOT

A few years into my medical practice, I met Pastor Antonio, a young man of about twenty-five years old. He was applying for the position of children's pastor at our church. As the parents of four youngsters, Lydia and I were part of the group tasked with interviewing various candidates.

The gregarious pastor wasn't slowed down by the fact that he weighed more than four hundred pounds. We met a couple of times, but then we didn't see each other for a while. When we did get together a few months later, his appearance had dramatically changed—he had shed more than a hundred pounds! Proud of his weight loss, he attributed it to dieting. However, he had a problem: he was still losing weight after coming off his diet. That was a red flag to me, suggesting something more serious was at play.

Curious about the hand towel around his neck, I asked why he wore it and discovered he was sweating so much it was needed to keep his clothes dry. As we talked, I learned he had another problem: a rapid heart rate that kept him up at night. Nervous energy made him feel unsettled and edgy, even irritable. I glanced down at his fingernails and saw they were separating from the nail beds. The diagnosis seemed obvious; a blood test confirmed it. He had too much thyroid hormone in his system, a condition known as "hyperthyroidism."

The thyroid gland secretes thyroid hormone into the bloodstream. This hormone is a vital resource for life; a balanced level is essential. Normally, the level is controlled through a "feedback loop"—similar to the way a thermostat establishes a constant room temperature. When the level in the blood drops too low, then more is provided by the thyroid gland. When it is too high, the gland produces less. A healthy thyroid gland senses feedback from the body continuously to provide just enough to maintain balance. Thyroid hormone is a good thing, but too much of a good thing can cause undesirable consequences.

Pastor Antonio's thyroid gland had become sick. Since it couldn't sense signals from the body that the levels of this resource were abnormally high, it kept right on working full throttle. And as a result, his body became more and more unhealthy.

Fortunately, medications were available to treat his condition. One blocked his excess hormone production, while a second addressed his rapid heart rate and other symptoms. Over time, his body returned to a normal balance. The last time I saw him, he was in good health.

Resources in Balance

Pastor Antonio's problem illustrates the need for a balance of resources in the body. An abnormally high thyroid hormone level caused his body to burn up calories faster than he could take them in, so he lost weight abnormally. His body's resources were squandered due to the imbalance.

In the same way, the body of Christ requires balance so it will have the resources it needs to grow, mature, and reproduce. As members of a living entity, we must strive to maintain balance and look to God to meet all our needs.

The healthy cells in your body demand a constant stream of nourishment as you go about your daily life. The amount of food you eat every day is generally in balance with the amount used up by your body. If you overeat, the excess resources are stored in your fat cells, and you gain weight. On the other hand, if you consume less than your body needs, then stored resources are used up, and you lose weight. In diseases like Antonio's hyperthyroidism, the metabolic rate is increased, and the balance between needs and resources becomes distorted. Resources are burned up at a much higher rate, so patients tend to lose weight as their disease advances, even when they continue to eat normally.

The inner workings of a living body are in balance. The term for this is homeostasis. Earlier, I remarked that the more I studied the body, the more intrigued I became. Homeostasis is one example of why I say that. The self-regulating systems that keep the body in the balance it needs to survive are—to use a phrase my kids would call antiquated—"mind blowing." When it's hot, you sweat. When it's cold, you shiver. You adjust to preserve the internal temperature you need to live, around 98.6 degrees Fahrenheit. Another example of homeostasis is the delicate balance of acids in the blood. Then there is the balancing of blood sugar levels. When you eat a big meal, your sugar level goes up, so your body adapts by producing more insulin to bring it down. If the level goes too low, your body adjusts by producing less insulin. It's a constant balancing act to keep things in equilibrium.

Our bodies use up a lot of resources just to maintain homeostasis. Given the ongoing shifts in their surroundings, they must constantly expend energy to maintain internal stability so we can continue with our daily activities. If our internal processes are less efficient, more resources will be needed to provide stability—something like a car needing more gas if its engine is poorly tuned. In the body of Christ, when we behave more like a nonliving organization, we must consume an inordinate amount of resources while attending to intrachurch squabbles. Provisions are squandered, and we become less able to cope with the challenges in the world around us. When we function more like members of a living body, though, fewer resources must be diverted to manage internal problems. Then the body of Christ can better address its mission in the world.

Because it is a living organism, the body of Christ must have a continuous provision of resources from God. He is able to, and will, satisfy all our needs. As Paul wrote: "And my God will meet all your needs according to the riches of his glory in Christ Jesus" (Philippians 4:19).

The Creator equips members of the body for ministry with the physical things we need, as well as with spiritual gifts. Paul outlined this in his first letter to the church at Corinth:

> To one there is given through the Spirit a message of wisdom, to another a message of knowledge by means of the same Spirit, to another faith by the same Spirit, to another gifts of healing by that one Spirit, to another miraculous powers, to another prophecy, to another distinguishing between spirits, to another speaking in different kinds of tongues, and to still another the interpretation of tongues. All these are the work of one and the same Spirit, and he distributes them to each one, just as he determines.
>
> —1 Corinthians 12:8–11

Each believer is given spiritual gifts. You cannot earn these through hard work; they come from God. Spiritual gifts are intended to build up the body, not its individual members. Granted, individuals may benefit as a side effect, but this is not the primary intent. Paul brought this out later in the same letter: "What then shall we say, brothers and sisters? When you come together, each of you has a hymn, or a word of instruction, a revelation, a tongue or an interpretation. Everything must be done so that the church may be built up" (1 Corinthians 14:26).

WE GROW

In the book of Acts, Luke chronicled how the first church developed rapidly as the members demonstrated love for one another: "Every day they continued to meet together in the temple courts. They broke bread in their homes and ate together with glad and sincere hearts, praising God and enjoying the favor of all the people. And the Lord added to their number daily those who were being saved" (Acts 2:46–47). Later, Luke records, "More and more men and women believed in the Lord and were added to their number" (Acts 5:14).

Material can be added to nonliving things—such as rocks—over time so they gradually increase in size. However, living things don't grow by merely accumulating more stuff on their bodies. They grow through a process called assimilation, which is much more involved than is ordinary addition. It happens when a living body absorbs material from the outside (i.e., food) and transforms it into living tissue (i.e., new cells).

Notice that the early believers did not just show up for Sunday services and live the remainder of the week as individuals. They regularly met together, ate together, owned possessions together, and developed a close-knit community. They also discipled and assimilated converts into the body. This is like the process in biology by which a living body takes in nonliving material and, through the process of assimilation, the material becomes a living part of the body. The mature believers disciple converts, who mature and eventually replace them at some point.

Another crucial point about assimilation is how it occurs from within the living body. You might say assimilation allows living things to "grow from the inside out." Addition occurs from the "outside in." Thus, assimilation may result in growth and development without an actual increase in overall body size.

Don't get carried away with the idea that unless your particular church is expanding, it is a failure. Remember that, in the world of biology, bigger isn't always better. For those suffering from cancer, an enlarged tumor is not a good sign. We sometimes take it for granted that a larger group is better and a smaller one is worse. But that's not always the case with living bodies.

Many tried-and-true strategies have been used to promote "church growth." Over the years, business, marketing, psychology, communications, and other fields have developed effective tools for business growth. They can provide results *if we are an organization* primarily focused on audience turnout. However, if we want to be more like a living body, then assimilation and discipleship are needed. Instead of asking, "How can we get more people into our church?" we might inquire, "How can we best grow and develop those already here?"

"Growth for growth's sake, man-made growth, can be spiritually deadening," conservative Catholic leader Reverend Richard Neuhaus told author Charles Colson in the award-winning book *The Body: Being Light in Darkness.* "Institutional growth is the last refuge of ministries that are spiritually sterile."[2]

WE MATURE

Our bodies use resources for more than just keeping things in balance. We also mature over time. All living things do this. This is another reality that makes up a part of the fingerprint of God and reveals a characteristic of His nature.

Unfortunately, I have treated diseases in which "renegade" cells decided not to mature in a healthy way. Something happened within them, and they exchanged the plan written in their DNA for a counterfeit. They became cancer. They did things their own way, rather than following God-given instructions for the good of the body. Subsequently, they threatened patients' lives.

The Bible is like the genetic code for the body of Christ. Members are intended to develop according to standards written in the Scriptures. Christ gives us different ministries to help the body mature, as shown in Paul's letter to the church at Ephesus:

> So Christ himself gave the apostles, the prophets, the evangelists, the pastors and teachers, to equip his people for works of service, so that the body of Christ may be built up until we all reach unity in the faith and in the knowledge of the Son of God and become mature, attaining to the whole measure of the fullness of Christ. Then we will no longer be infants, tossed back and forth by the waves, and blown here and there by every wind of teaching and by the cunning and craftiness of people in their deceitful scheming.
>
> —EPHESIANS 4:11–14

Just as a farmer discerns what conditions are necessary to grow a crop from seed, God knows precisely what we require to fulfill our destiny in the body of Christ. He has not only created us as unique individuals but put each of us in a particular time and place for the body. Since He knows that every living body requires food, Christ ensures there is adequate nutrition for our development. He cares for His body. As Peter noted in his second epistle, "His divine power has given us everything we need for a godly life through our knowledge of him who called us by his own glory and goodness" (2 Peter 1:3).

Scripture exhorts us again and again not just to remain static in our development but to grow and mature over time:

- In 1 Corinthians 3, Paul writes to the church, "Brothers and sisters, I could not address you as people who live by the Spirit but as people who are still worldly—mere infants in Christ. I gave you milk, not solid food, for you were not yet ready for it. Indeed, you are still not ready" (1 Corinthians 3:1–2).

- Hebrews encourages Christians to keep up their spiritual training: "In fact, though by this time you ought to be teachers, you need someone to teach you the elementary truths of God's word all over again. You need milk, not solid food! Anyone who lives on milk, being still an infant, is not acquainted with the teaching about righteousness. But solid food is for the mature, who by constant use have trained themselves to distinguish good from evil" (Hebrews 5:12–14).

- And Peter tells Christians what they must do to mature in the faith, saying, "Therefore, rid yourselves of all malice and all deceit, hypocrisy, envy, and slander of every kind. Like newborn babies, crave pure spiritual milk, so that by it you may grow up in your salvation, now that you have tasted that the Lord is good" (1 Peter 2:1–3).

WE REPRODUCE

Growth and development in a living body means that individual members mature to the point that they are productive. Cells in a healthy body don't keep enlarging indefinitely but bring forth "children." Living bodies grow as individual cells (or members) mature and develop new cells (or members). Sometimes we think of church growth as the process of adding people from other congregations to ours. But that resembles the way a nonliving rock increases in size through addition. A healthy church will assimilate nonbelievers and help them develop into fully devoted followers of Christ.

Reproduction is a characteristic of living bodies. It is a component of the fingerprint of God and expresses an aspect of His nature. Things made by man do not reproduce as a living body. For instance, a coffee-maker can make coffee, but not additional coffee makers. Coffee plants can reproduce more coffee plants, though, because God created them, and they are living bodies.

Living organisms grow new cells to replace worn-out cells. An individual cell reproduces by dividing into two new cells. Just before it splits, parts double up within the parent cell. During this time, there are—in effect—twice the functioning parts enclosed within the parent. The offspring tend to develop all the characteristics of the parent and then eventually produce their own offspring.

In the case of cancer, the cells of a malignant tumor draw vital resources away from the healthy cells to reproduce cancer cells at an unsustainable pace. In the body of Christ, we must be aware of the biblical standards by which we are to live. If we throw off restraint and try to replicate what is nonbiblical, the entire body will suffer.

It is important to distinguish between reproduction and division. When nonliving things divide without reproducing, they are less than they were before. Dividing, as exemplified by church splits, is not a favorable method for reproduction of such living organisms as the body of Christ.

While it is normal for cells to make cell parts, evangelists to make converts, and leaders to make followers, these processes are not the same as reproduction, which is a vital process for the body of Christ. It means an evangelist makes a new evangelist (not a new convert). A leader reproduces by creating a new leader (not a new follower). We disciple others to rise up and take our place when we are gone.

ALL LIFE COMES FROM PREEXISTING LIFE

No matter which patients I examine, there is a universal truth regarding the origination of all the cells in their bodies—they all came from preexisting life. The cells originated from other cells, generation after generation. Scientists call this *biogenesis*. The living God is ultimately the originator of all life. Paul wrote this to Timothy (1 Timothy 6:13).

As I write these words, I know of experimenters around the world trying to create life out of nonliving materials. However, I don't think they will ever be able to manufacture a living being. While it is true that man-made objects may exhibit some qualities of life, they are not living unless they wholly express the qualities of life. It seems that only God can do this; as Paul told the Greek philosophers on Mars Hill: "'For in him we live and move and have our being.' As some of your own poets have said, 'We are his offspring'" (Acts 17:28). As the offspring of God, we can have assurance that He will meet all our needs.

QUESTIONS FOR DISCUSSION

1. Have you ever seen a "miraculous" healing? How do you feel about the possibility of such healings?
2. The Creator equips us for ministry with our physical requirements, as well as with spiritual gifts. How should you use your spiritual gifts?
3. Living things don't grow merely by accumulating material. They absorb material and assimilate it into living cells for the body. What do you think this means for growth in the living body of Christ?
4. How is the Bible like the genetic code for the body of Christ?
5. Growth and development in things made by God include maturity of individual members to the point they can have "children." Things made by man do not do this. What can we learn from the differences between a coffeemaker and a coffee tree?
6. How do you think we can be unified as the living body of Christ? Do you think this is even possible?

CHAPTER
8

CELLS: THE MEMBERS OF THE BODY

The key is that life does not simply reduce down to transcribing static passages from our genetic scripture. Cells figure out which passages to pay attention to by observing signals from the cells around them: only with that local interaction can complex "neighborhoods" of cell types come into being . . . Cells rely heavily on the code of DNA for development, but they also need a sense of place to do their work. Indeed, the code is utterly worthless without the cell's ability to determine its place in the overall organism, a feat that is accomplished by the elegant strategy of paying attention to one's neighbors . . . Since every cell in the body carries a complete copy of the genome, no cell need wait for instructions from authority; every cell can act on its own information and the signals it receives from its neighbors.[1]

—AUTHOR STEVEN JOHNSON

His name was Johnny. Back in the 1980s, a homosexual man suffering from AIDS invited scorn, condemnation, and silent suffering. After years of the ravages of this disease, his body had become a frail specimen. On this latest admission, he had pancytopenia (very low blood cell counts), bacterial sepsis (a serious infection), and presumably PCP (a type of pneumonia). To make matters worse, he then developed Stevens-Johnson syndrome as an unintended side effect of the medications we used to treat his infection. A rare, serious disorder of the skin and mucous membranes, it starts with flu-like symptoms and is often followed by a painful red or purplish rash that spreads and blisters. In Johnny's case, the disorder caused his skin to gradually fall off of his body. The lining of his mouth and lips also peeled off. He became an oozing mass of human flesh (which made it especially unappealing to care for him, considering AIDS is contagious and spreads through body fluids).

During my medical training, HIV and AIDS were newcomers on the horizon. Thanks to recently developed treatments and medications, these conditions are much more manageable today. Yet back then, physicians were quite limited in the options we had to offer these patients. It was heartbreaking to watch AIDS patients like Johnny deteriorate and die. I cared for him on a daily basis for weeks. Because of his disease and the pain medications we had prescribed, he would often become incoherent. When he had his mental faculties, I would sometimes talk with him and his friends. Over time, he and I developed a friendship.

Something about Johnny has stayed with me, even though he died years ago. In spite of his horrible physical condition, he showed concern for my feelings and my welfare.

It saddens me to think of the times I was too repulsed by the lifestyle of my AIDS patients to see beyond that and show compassion for them as people. Sadly, in an age when the issue of advancing gay rights has driven an even deeper wedge between the respective supporters and opponents, too many Christians allow their political vision to cloud their humanity.

Even more troubling than the fact that Johnny died a horrible death was that he did so in an unrepentant state. The same day I pronounced Johnny dead, another homosexual patient of mine with AIDS also died. Yet this man—ironically also named Johnny—had become a Christian. His death scene stood in stark contrast to the unrepentant patient. The second Johnny's entire family gathered at his bedside for a home-going vigil characterized by an atmosphere of peace, prayer, and Bible reading. I'll never forget the experience of being in that room.

These two men had the same name, the same disease, the same doctor, were in the same hospital, and passed away the same day. They died under very different conditions, though. One perceived AIDS as only a physical issue that hindered his lifestyle. At the time of his death, the other saw beyond his natural state to the wonders of the supernatural realm.

JOINING OTHER CELLS

Before departing from this world, the second Johnny connected with the body of Christ. He never joined a church, entered the baptismal pool, completed a new believers' class, or shared his testimony with a congregation. His entrance into heaven, though, was every bit as certain as that of the thief on the cross who acknowledged Jesus's authority even as he hung beside him (Luke 23:39–43).

The fact that Christ welcomed such a man into eternity despite a lifetime of criminal activity demonstrates His forgiveness, acceptance, and willingness to forgive anyone who accepts Him as Savior. In so doing, all who believe in Jesus become part of a body that functions in ways similar to the cells that make up our physical body. All living bodies are composed of cells. The smallest of organisms, such as bacteria, have only one cell. They are so tiny they cannot be seen with the unaided eye. Other organisms are huge by comparison and are composed of billions of cells.

Cells within a body have various sizes and shapes, depending on what they are called on to do for the body. The size of an organism is generally not due to the size of its cells but rather the number of cells it contains. When a cell reaches a certain level of maturity, it is natural for it to divide into two new cells, each with the characteristics of the parent cell. This reproductive division can be done only when the parent cell is mature enough to divide into two self-sustaining cells.

Your body consists of members called cells. The body of Christ consists of members called believers. Because believers are like cells, let's look at the genetic composition of the body's cells and see what we can learn about the body of Christ. It starts with DNA—short for deoxyribonucleic acid, the special molecules that give us our genetic code.

DNA is so special because it reflects the fact that God wrote a unique code for each one of us. You literally are one of a kind! Your body contains about 260 different types of cells, each of which possesses a complete copy of the genetic code for your entire body. Your code is physically inscribed on your DNA using a four-letter alphabet. I don't know why God chose to use only four letters, but they are what scientists consistently identify in all living things. With the aid of a microscope, you can actually see what God has written about you in your DNA molecules. He wrote the language of life with these four chemical letters:

A = an adenine molecule
C = a cytosine molecule
T = a thymine molecule
G = a guanine molecule

DNA consists of a long string of these letters written in such a way as to create the code of life. The author of life wrote it in a language understandable by all your cells, providing physical proof that you were first conceived in the mind of the author and that your life has purpose. Just look at the way billions of these four letters are strung out in a line of code to form groups, similar to words and sentences. Like the rules in a game, your genetic code provides a blueprint for each cell to follow. Your cells don't use the entire code all the time. They use the part of the code written for each situation. They discern which part to use by sensing their location in the body and what other cells around them are communicating. It's vital that cells pay attention to this information.

A cell is not required to await new instructions. It just uses the genetic directions it already has, along with signals from neighboring cells and information about the surroundings. A healthy cell pays keen attention to its neighbors and uses the communication it receives from them. While cells in a living body can handle numerous tasks, an individual cell does not accomplish all these tasks by itself. In fact, in a complex organism like the human body, some cells are specialized and perform only a few specific tasks. The different types of cells need to work in unity to be a living body.

THE GENETIC CODE

How does knowing all this benefit us as members of the living body of Christ? Through recognizing that God provides written instructions for every cell in this spiritual body to live by: His Word, written in the Bible. This book contains instructions for each member, yet it isn't all-inclusive for every particular situation we encounter. We use the Bible in combination with our interactions with other believers, much as a cell knows to use specific sections of the DNA code by its interactions with neighboring cells. This is how a seed becomes a flower. The DNA contains patterns to follow.

The Bible gives us a standard by which to live in every situation, depending on our location in the body, our relationships with other members, and the circumstances surrounding us in the world. It is vital that we follow the Bible as our standard. Moreover, it is vital that we nurture relationships with other believers around us and have a biblical perspective about the worldly environment in which we live.

We also should be aware of the nature of diseases, because nearly every physical illness is related to a malfunction of the cells. In the same way, almost every problem in the body of Christ is related to a malfunction of its cells (members). Look at the following examples:

1. **Immune Diseases**

   One type of immune disease causes the body to be overly aggressive and attack other parts of the body as if they were foreign invaders. Rheumatoid arthritis is an example of such a disease.

   When we harbor traits like unforgiveness against others in the body of Christ—causing us to attack them—we are attacking ourselves and causing pain and disability to all.

2. **Infection**

   This occurs when foreign germs containing foreign DNA invade the body. These germs reproduce themselves, destroying the cells with which they come into contact. The body has an immune system to recognize this threat in the early stages—hopefully before the infection causes too much damage. The immune system fights this battle by distinguishing self from nonself. In other words, it defines which cells are part of the body and which cells are not, working to neutralize substances that should not be present.

As members of the body of Christ, we are in the world but not of the world. This means we must exercise spiritual discernment so that the worldly culture in which we live does not invade the body and cause problems. Discernment in any situation means ascertaining whether or not the Bible forms the standard by which we seek to live. Many popular causes, theories, and philosophies are directly opposite of Scripture.

3. Cancer

This occurs when an otherwise normal cell develops a different code in its DNA, causing its growth and reproduction to spin out of control. Cancer cells invade nearby healthy cells, causing them to die. They may even metastasize to distant parts of the body, where they continue to wreak havoc there as well. Paradoxically, by throwing off restraint and promoting themselves, cancer cells ensure their own eventual demise, along with that of others.

Likewise, when believers ignore the Word and promote themselves at the expense of healthy doctrine or the well-being of others (whether within a local congregation or the wider body of Christ), they may seem to initially follow a successful path. Their TV program, book, curriculum, or other initiative may prosper. But if doing so inflicts harm, causes others to doubt their faith, or brings disrepute to the church as a whole, the net effect can resemble cancer. Ultimately, they are ensuring the demise of themselves and others while causing pain and disability in the body.

MENTORING IN THE BODY

Just as physical diseases have parallels in the body of Christ, so too do many of the more healthy qualities. Take mentoring, for example. While this has served as a modern buzzword, its roots are found in the physical body. You began life as a single cell, with half of your DNA coming from your father and half from your mother. This single cell divided into two; two cells became four; four became eight, eight became sixteen, and so on. Rapid growth brought about the right conditions for the cells to develop along different paths. Each cell determined where it was located in the overall body and developed as necessary for the good of the whole. One cell became a blood cell, another a muscle cell, another a lung cell, and so on.

How did your cells establish their position in the body and follow the right developmental path? There was no "bird's-eye view" for the cells. They determined their position and function through a kind of mentoring—namely, communication with neighboring cells and the cues this interchange provided. Then groups of these cells came together to form a bone, a brain, or another organ. Once this differentiation took place in your body, the subsequent cells remained essentially unchanged in their type. Cellular function is handed down from one generation to the next.

In the same way that cells work together and grow, pastors are called to mentor younger believers to become future pastors in the body of Christ. Apostles, prophets, evangelists, and teachers are to do the same. The Bible describes several ministry functions for members of the body of Christ. An individual member may function in several areas or in only one, depending on the situation. To quote a passage I mentioned earlier: "So Christ himself gave the apostles, the prophets, the evangelists, the pastors and teachers, to equip his people for works of service, so that the body of Christ may be built up" (Ephesians 4:11–12).

This mentor-based reality shows that our confidence in the body of Christ should not rest on sterling speakers; superstar ministers, authors, singers, and actors; or famous personalities exercising special spiritual gifts that only a rare few possess. We follow the same life cycle as cells do. They are born, fulfill their roles in the body, reproduce, and finally die. Their life span is typically short compared with that of the body as a whole. What does this mean for us as members of the living body of Christ? The body of Christ was born on Easter; we as members were "reborn" at a later point in history. We have a relatively short life span compared with the body as a whole. God has placed us at a particular time and place in the body. We should give our full devotion to fulfilling our role in the short time we have. We should also mentor other, younger believers as the opportunity arises so that they will be healthy members of the body after we are gone.

THE ART OF ADAPTATION

Just as cells grow, subdivide, and multiply in creating a healthy body, God created our physical body with the ability to adapt to changing circumstances. Adaptation is a dynamic, ongoing, life-sustaining process by which living organisms adjust to their environment. Life requires that a body change in response to changing conditions. Lack of adaptation results in death.

I occasionally see ER patients who (for various reasons) have lost the ability to thermoregulate, meaning they can no longer adapt to environmental conditions and maintain a normal body temperature. One in particular was on his first day out harvesting crops on a very hot summer day. He was not acclimated to the heat. Over a few hours, his body temperature had risen to such a point that he had lost consciousness and his organs had begun to fail. When paramedics brought him to me, his temperature had risen to more than 108 degrees. It took quick action to save his life.

At the other extreme was the young man who fell into a lake in subfreezing weather. Because of difficulties getting to him, he lay underwater and didn't breathe for at least thirty minutes. His body temperature rapidly approached that of the cold lake water as his ability to thermoregulate shut down. When he arrived at the ER, his heart was not beating; he had not been breathing for some time. Fortunately, his cold body temperature had helped preserve his organs enough that we were able to revive him.

Just as our bodies maintain a normal temperature and resist becoming one with the environment, members of the body of Christ are called to be in the world but not of it. History teaches that Christian groups or denominations, no matter how sincere and alive, can, over time, become influenced by the world and conform to it. We need wisdom to survive in the world without becoming part of it.

CONSUMER MENTALITY

While much of the church-growth movement sprang from legitimate concerns with strengthening the church's influence in the world, it has had unintended consequences. The modern church has invested countless hours in becoming the best organization it can be by using the best business practices possible. However, God intended for us to become a living body, not a business. When we follow the ways of the world, we wind up creating a consumer mentality among those who come to the church.

Remember the old saying "the customer is always right"? That tagline bothered me, even in my childhood, because I knew it could not be true. Granted, it was a way to help employees remember their duty to serve the customer. But that philosophy has fatal consequences for churches, especially when they allow potential customers to drive their decision-making. Take the practice of churches conducting marketing surveys to determine what characteristics people in certain neighborhoods want in a church and then using that information to determine the congregation's identity. Although I understand the need to be friendly and responsive, allowing the desires of potential "customers"—instead of Scripture and prayer—to drive decision-making is akin to having an infection in the body. We will discuss this in more detail in chapter 12.

What's worse is the way this customer-service trend has created an entertainment mentality in the church. Because people want to be entertained, churches provide entertainment, and as technology progresses, the entertainment tends to become more and more extravagant. While drawing a crowd may not be inherently bad, amid the lights, sounds, glitter, and video production, it is too easy to lose sight of what is truly important. Jesus did not perform a song-and-dance routine to gather a crowd; He taught the truth. The crowds naturally followed.

This is why Paul wrote that members of the body of Christ should not become one with the world, instructing the church in Rome, "Do not conform to the pattern of this world, but be transformed by the renewing of your mind. Then you will be able to test and approve what God's will is—his good, pleasing and perfect will" (Romans 12:2).

THE BODY'S VARIABILITY

Moderate Variability

(6–25 bpm variation around baseline)

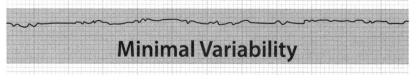

Minimal Variability

(<5 bpm variation around baseline)

Absent Variability

(No detectable variation around baseline)

These charts illustrate that we can diagram changes in how fast a heart is beating. Unevenness shows a heart making healthy adjustments to changes in the environment. An unchanging heart rate may indicate disease and approaching death. Ironically, the heart rate that appears the steadiest is, in reality, the most unstable and dangerous for life.

This is true of more than the heart. As Pastor Antonio learned, a healthy thyroid gland secretes more or less hormone depending on what the body needs at the time. Your stomach cells make more or less acid for digestion based on whether food is present, and so on. Human beings have designed their machines with this principle in mind. Rudders on ships are made to be movable, to respond to changes on the water so that the boat as a whole remains safe. When you drive a car on a perfectly straight and level road, you can't just take your hands off of the steering wheel. You still have to make small adjustments left and right. Airline flights make minor course changes constantly; to remain true to their overall course, they must adjust, or they will miss their target.

Adjustments are needed for stability. This may seem counterintuitive since we think of stability as something rigid and unchanging, but living organisms are constantly making adjustments, continuously changing. This is part of the dynamic nature of the universe and of living organisms in particular. The changes that take place in living organisms occur according to the season, the time, or the demands placed on the body. At times, different challenges are placed on the body. Thus, the individual parts are required to adjust what they do depending on the situation at hand. But keep in mind that living bodies adjust to live, not as a means of becoming one with the world.

Living bodies are agile and adaptable. How can this type of flexibility come from an inflexible set of rules like the genetic code written in our DNA? The paradox in living bodies is that flexibility emerges from rigid rules. There are no exceptions. This principle exists within the body of Christ, too, in which unchanging laws (i.e., the Ten Commandments) let us experience life and freedom to the fullest. Unbending rules permit us to have freedom. That which restrains us actually gives us life. I like the way David put it in this Psalm: "Lord, you alone are my portion and my cup; you make my lot secure. *The boundary lines have fallen for me in pleasant places*; surely I have a delightful inheritance" (Psalm 16:5–6, emphasis added).

Living bodies are by nature complex. Yet when we strip away the layers of complexity, sooner or later, we discover utter simplicity in the set of rules that governs life. Through an amazing plan created by God, a flexible organism arises from inflexible components. We are free to drive our lives almost anywhere as long as we stay on the road. He puts guardrails along the sides of the road so we will be awakened to our errors before we careen too far off the road. In His plan, freedom is necessarily coupled with responsibility. Contrary to popular opinion, freedom does not mean an absence of rules. Rules enable reaction to the circumstances that arise in life; rules permit a healthy self-regulation to the environment around us. Right rules allow us to live in true freedom.

LEARNING FROM THE PAST

Adaptation works through looking backward to the past for guidance, because it is impossible to gaze into the future for advice. In other words, the body adjusts to environmental shifts and changes by looking at what we have been exposed to previously. This works well when the environment is calm. Times of turbulent change can overwhelm us if we are unable to respond quickly, though.

You should never grow discouraged when you try and fail; success can be a two-edged sword. Early successes in life can actually handicap us for the future. For instance, when we have succeeded in a task, we may be slow to make necessary adjustments later. We can get stuck in a rut and "locked in" to routines that would better serve us if we made adjustments along the way. On the other hand, early failures can increase later successes by forcing us to become more flexible in our methods.

A living body's ability to adjust is even more critical for survival when the environment is unstable. At the same time, it must preserve sufficient order to maintain its vital processes. Too much rigidity stifles adjustment and ends in death. Too much flexibility generates chaos and ends in death. The living body must find a "sweet spot" between these two extremes.

As for life in the body of Christ, culture and traditions can flavor our faith and intermix in our minds to the point that we cannot differentiate between what is biblical and what is religious (or cultural) tradition. We must be careful to not compromise our core principles yet remain flexible when differences of opinion arise about traditions or other issues that are not at the core of the Christian faith. Name any contentious issue—whether it is singing traditional or contemporary hymns, which

Bible translation is the best, or which day of the week we must worship—and it is quite often superfluous to the body's primary task.

As we contend with our ever-changing world, the issue we must face is if we will perceive these changes as a threat or as an opportunity. Rather than getting mired in lamenting the disappearance of the "good old days" or whining about Christianity losing its favored status in America, we may learn to appreciate the fact that perhaps the richest environment for the will of God to come about in today's world is a changing and shifting one. Having the mind of Christ can promote more innovation and opportunity instead of regressive outlooks or attempts to reinvent the 1950s (an era whose *Leave It to Beaver* image was a myth anyway).

Some people claim the definition of insanity is repeating a failed activity over and over, hoping for a different result. Instead of following the same old path, we need to be wise and adjust appropriately for a glorious future in God's kingdom. Man-made organizations tend to be geared for the status quo, always nervous about change and reluctant to march into the future. Fueled by adaptation, living bodies are always ready for changing conditions. They look to the future as they are guided by past experiences.

QUESTIONS FOR DISCUSSION

1. All living bodies on earth are composed of cells. The body of Christ is composed of believers. What can we learn about our role in the body of Christ by studying cells?

2. God physically wrote your one-of-a-kind genetic code on your DNA in a language understandable by the cells in your body. How does knowing this help you better understand that He has a plan for your life?

3. While a healthy cell follows its genetic code to the letter, it still pays keen attention to signals from its neighbors and uses the communication it receives from them. What does this say about how members of the body of Christ are to relate to the Bible? To other believers?

4. Cancer forms when an otherwise normal cell develops a different code in its DNA, causing growth and reproduction to spin out of control. How might this compare with those who value growth in their Christian ministry at the expense of deviating from Scripture?

5. Infection occurs when germs containing a foreign genetic code invade the body and propagate. How might this compare with allowing the ways of the world into the body of Christ?

6. A weakened immune system can cause the body to be too weak and allow invading germs in the body. But an overactive system can attack other members of the body as if they were invaders. What does this say about the need for discernment and charity in the body of Christ?

7. Heart, lung, and other types of cells produce the same kinds of cells while passing down their roles from one generation to the next. What does this say about the value of mentoring?

CHAPTER
9

UNITY AMID DIVERSITY

*We are to be stewards of the unique design and motivation that
God has placed on our hearts. Instead of filling a church slot as
defined by the institution, an organism seeks to have each person
play the part for which he or she was created. A church's ministry
takes the shape of the gifted people instead of forcing the people
into preexisting niches that act like a confining straitjacket.*[1]

—GREG OGDEN, *UNFINISHED BUSINESS*

With flat-screen televisions hanging everywhere—whether in airports or
at the corner grocery store—and millions checking out video clips or live
telecasts on their smartphones, we can get so accustomed to watching
political rallies that they become one more ho-hum experience. But the
time I attended a campaign rally for a presidential hopeful several years
ago, the atmosphere sizzled with electricity. More than four thousand
people had crowded into the auditorium and buzzed excitedly as they
waited for the candidate to appear. In this Southern city, it seemed everyone knew everyone, prompting considerable "Hey, how are yous?"
and quick selfies.

No sooner had the host started introductions than there was a stir in
the crowd. Leaning over to the microphone, the host announced, "We
have a medical emergency. A doctor is needed as soon as possible in the
rear hallway."

Glancing around at the area, I saw people gathering around a man
lying face up in the aisle, about twenty rows back from where I sat. I
rushed to the long aisle, stepping on as few people's feet as possible, in

a hurry to reach the unresponsive guest. Looking around and seeing that no one else was providing emergency care, I bent down to check for a pulse and respirations. Nothing. His chest lay silent. Immediately, I started CPR, administering mouth-to-mouth resuscitation and chest compressions. Meanwhile, my brain raced as I mentally prepared for the possibilities: heart attack, pulmonary embolism, heart rhythm problem, or some other deadly ailment. As I worked, I thought about not being licensed to practice medicine in this state. Fortunately, there are "Good Samaritan" laws that give us the freedom to act in a patient's best interest in an emergency even without the proper credentials.

Offering this kind of aid might seem routine for a doctor; I had delivered this type of assistance countless times in the ER. But this was my first time "in the field," where I had no medications or equipment by my side. Nor had I ever held up a presidential candidate's rally. As what I thought would be a five-minute wait for paramedics turned into twenty, I felt sweat drenching my armpits and trickling down my eyebrows. Doing chest compressions is taxing enough, but I also sensed the awkwardness of what felt like more than eight thousand eyes staring in my direction. When a commotion sounded and I saw several paramedics scampering up the aisle, I breathed a sigh of relief. They shocked his heart back into rhythm before loading him onto a stretcher and taking him to the ambulance outside. He never regained consciousness at the scene. Unfortunately, I later heard secondhand that he lived for only a few more days.

CREATING A BODY

You might suspect that most doctors, who need a calming bedside manner and the ability to deal with a wide variety of patients, possess a gregarious, outgoing nature. As you can tell from my sweaty reaction to a very public emergency, this is not always the case. Because I am a rather private person, it is difficult for me to open up in conversation with others. So, when I first understood that we are called to be one body, I struggled with the idea. *Me, intimately connected with every other Christian in the world? Surely God doesn't mean we are to make ourselves that vulnerable!* The thought conflicted with my strong sense of individualism and instinctive resistance to the notion of "oneness."

Nor did the outcomes from programs seeking to unify Christian denominations, whether on a national or a worldwide basis, inspire much confidence. I had seen others who embraced even broader agendas, such as attempting to unify followers of all religions. I likened these endeavors to assembling a sort of Frankenstein's monster, sewn together from parts of different cadavers that were never meant to mesh. Such efforts have never come close to creating unity. Yet I now realize that this is not what the Bible calls unity of the body. The unity described in Scripture suggests we are intimately interconnected with one another on a deep, spiritual level, unseen by those who seek to organize the body of Christ using human methods.

Indeed, spiritual unity is the structural essence of the body of Christ. It's as Paul wrote to the Corinthians: "But God has put the body together, giving greater honor to the parts that lacked it, so that there should be no division in the body, but that its parts should have equal concern for each other. If one part suffers, every part suffers with it; if one part is honored, every part rejoices with it." (1 Corinthians 12:24–26).

However, unity does not imply conformity. Organizations may promote conformity through rigid guidelines, often using fear as a motivating factor. In contrast, the body of Christ promotes unity through vision and faith, but room for diversity is preserved. We may instinctively want other believers to look like us, act like us, and conform to our religious ideas, but we were not created to be identical.

We can live without an eye or a hand, but we cannot live without some of the other, less obvious body parts, such as a functioning pancreas or lymphatic system. Our less prestigious parts are often more necessary. Because we are members of a body, none of us is complete by ourselves. The Creator made each of us as unique but imperfect individuals.

Maintaining Unity

It is interesting to note that Paul did not tell believers to create unity but to maintain it. Humans cannot create unity; it is a gift from God.

He instructs us to keep and preserve unity through the bond of peace. The bonds among believers are similar to the bonds among cells in a body, which I reviewed in the previous chapter. Like cells, we need one another—deeply. The love that binds us together is stronger than the distinctions that separate us. The bonds among members of the body of Christ are stronger than other bonds that hold groups of people together, like nationality, race, or religious group. This is the kind of unity the first-century church modeled, as described in the first chapters of Acts.

After the day of Pentecost, the early church fellowshipped together in one another's homes, held things in common, and saw God's power working in their midst. This gives us a powerful picture of Christian unity—the kind demonstrated by the sacrament of communion. Communion not only is an opportunity to remember Christ's death (and resurrection) but is meant to be taken in community. It is far more than a mystical sacrament between individual believers and Christ. It is a time of sharing with other believers and relating to them.

From a biblical perspective, self-sufficiency is not our goal; as members of the body, we need one another. We are not well rounded and complete alone. The people you think are well rounded are undoubtedly rough in areas; you just haven't seen them yet. Besides, we should not strive to become self-reliant members of the body of Christ. Attempting it means separation and eventual death. After all, we can't say, "I'm healthy; it's just my stomach that's sick," or, "I feel no pain; it's just my leg that hurts." When one member suffers, we all suffer. When one rejoices, we all rejoice. We are one body.

FUNCTIONING AS A UNIT

Living bodies function as a unified whole. As I observed in chapter 4, members of a body cannot be easily disbanded or removed without causing trauma, while parts of a machine or members of a team usually can. The form of a body is brought about only by the physical presence of its members, and the actions of a body come about just through the interactions between and among all the constituent members. This happens over time and in continuously changing circumstances during the lifetime of the body. The importance of interaction among the members cannot be overstated. The behavior of the body as a whole emerges from these interactions.

A believer is not connected to Christ as an individual but as a body member. There is no painless escape from this body. Division is often compared to divorce. But it is more like dismemberment than divorce. We all desperately need one another. Members cannot live if severed from the body; they will rot.

As I reviewed in chapter 8, your body contains an assortment of cells under one genetic code—an example of unity amid diversity. The body of Christ contains this same unity amid diversity. We are an assortment of members under one head. A combination of unity and diversity makes for a healthy body.

DIVERSITY IN THE BODY

The diversity in the Church is another distinguishing feature of the fingerprint of God. Paul taught this truth in Romans when he compared the members of the body of Christ to members of a human body:

> For just as each of us has one body with many members, and these members do not all have the same function, so in Christ we, though many, form one body, and each member belongs to all the others. We have different gifts, according to the grace given to each of us. If your gift is prophesying, then prophesy in accordance with your faith; if it is serving, then serve; if it is teaching, then teach; if it is to encourage, then give encouragement; if it is giving, then give generously; if it is to lead, do it diligently; if it is to show mercy, do it cheerfully.
> —Romans 12:4–8

We can appreciate the need for diversity in contemplating the varying styles of worship in churches. What some believers consider unnecessary emotionalism others see as anointed and empowering ministry. What some people think is dead formalism or tradition others see as connecting them to the church throughout the ages. Their rituals may provide those particular worshipers stability, comfort, and a sense of awe as they contemplate God. Each perspective has its place in the body. We need to be careful not to put other believers in a box. In the body of Christ, there is room for wide diversity among people and local congregational styles.

But we also need to be careful not to allow our culture and traditions to taint our faith over time. They can become so intermixed in our minds that we cannot differentiate between orthodox Christianity and religious tradition. We must be careful not to compromise our core Christian principles yet remain flexible when differences of opinion arise over traditions or other issues that are not at the core of our Christian faith. Examine any church split, and you are more likely to encounter power struggles and personal preferences behind the conflict than honest differences regarding biblical doctrine.

In addition, some of the doctrinal disputes we frown on may actually serve a purpose. No member or group of members can claim to have achieved divine omniscience. We all see reality through the lens of our limited perspective. Doctrinal disputes often point out the fact that we all have a different angle of vision as we behold the truth.

All living things are diverse. A living body can't be uniform throughout. In order to live, its many different members must play different roles. As I have mentioned previously, we have a natural tendency to want other Christians to look and act like us and to conform to our religious ideas. But we weren't created to be identical; each of us is unique. This diversity forms a healthy body.

DEATHLY LACK OF CONFLICT

If we assembled together identical members in a church, the group would never be able to function as a normal body. There *would be* a lack of conflict, which might look calm and stable on the surface. However, this quality *would not be positive*. Instead of reflecting unity, it would mean the absence of the basic give-and-take functions of close relationships.

Rather than reflecting good health, this lack of conflict would signal that the church was not alive. The more diverse the members of an organism, the better it is able to function. Still, there must also be clear vision and focused leadership to keep the members aimed toward a higher calling and not going their own way.

The body of Christ contains individuals who might otherwise seem incompatible. Such a body forces me to interact with people whom I otherwise would not seek out. It doesn't resemble our concept of marriage; we don't get to choose the other people in the body. God's intention is for everyone to become a member. The broad assortment of gifts lets us know God plans for us to reach out into the full range of human activities.

Because we are members of a body, none of us is complete by ourselves. In making each of us unique, the Creator forces us to need one another. God created each of us uniquely to play specific roles. Some possess a gift in one area and some in another. No single individual is an expert in every gift of the Spirit. No one effectively ministers in all ministries. Because each member has a unique set of God-given abilities and experiences, every person possesses a perspective none of the other members possess. Each of us also has human limitations, meaning we need each other to better understand truth as well. We need one another's abilities to carry out Christ's ongoing ministry in this world.

This all comes wrapped in a package of peculiarities. Some members of this body are aggressive or loud. Some are quiet or so sensitive that others feel that they must walk on eggshells in their presence. We need to tolerate whatever idiosyncrasies or peculiar traits exist in other members, even if they try our patience (and remember, we may well try theirs). What seems less useful now may become vital in the future, when what once appeared annoying will suddenly be valuable. Take the crude oil lying under the sands of the Middle East. Prior to the invention of the internal combustion engine, this black goo appeared to be a worthless nuisance. In a similar manner, many characteristics in a species that seem eccentric or meaningless became quite useful in a different environment or time period.

None of us can fully know what God has called other members to do. Unless their behavior is clearly contrary to scriptural guidelines, we must be careful not to judge whether or not they are doing what God has called them to do. You can rest assured there is no one else like you—no one who thinks exactly as you do, has feelings exactly like yours, or possesses the same spiritual gifts as you do. No one can take your place in the body. You are an integral part of the divine plan for mankind. None of us should be in competition with one another because none of us can take the place of another member.

Yet while God calls each of us to be ministers, we do not all have the same ministry. There is infinite variety in our gifts and ministries. Still, there is always a core unity. In spite of the fact that we all have various functions in the body, our relationship with Christ does not differ. The hand relates to the head the same way the eye relates to the head. All of us are blessed with the same relationship to Christ through our spiritual rebirth.

USING SPIRITUAL GIFTS

Not only does each of us have unique gifts and talents, but God designed us to use them to meet one another's needs—and those of the world. We are to recognize our individual gifts and put them to use for the good of the body. The body of Christ is perfected when members neither neglect nor think too highly of their gifts. When the Bible mentions the gifts of the Spirit, it emphasizes that God has provided gifts to each member. We do not work up or create these spiritual gifts through our own efforts. They are from God, who gives them to us as He sees fit. None of us is without gifts, even though they might not be in use at all times. Most importantly, gifts are for the good of the body, not to edify the person using the gift. As Paul told the Corinthians: "There are different kinds of service, but the same Lord. There are different kinds of working, but in all of them and in everyone it is the same God at work. Now to each one the manifestation of the Spirit is given for the common good" (1 Corinthians 12:5–7).

The spiritual gifts we have as individuals do not mean we possess vast wisdom or proficiency. Above all, our spiritual gifts are the ways the

Holy Spirit Himself chooses to act in us. Given this reality, boasting or coveting the gifts of others is not just unproductive; it is grossly counter-productive. Every gift is needed for the healthy functioning of the body. So, we should take care not to place special status on a particular gift or on those who possess a gift we admire or desire for ourselves so we can "shine" in front of a crowd.

If we operate from a body-of-Christ perspective, we will not rank our spiritual gifts. Scripture does not place a hierarchy on gifts. We need to avoid mimicking others whom we admire and instead develop our own unique gifts. If we reduce the gifts of members to a list we are craving, then the diverse members are not all presented, and the health of the whole body is at stake. Just as we shouldn't copy other people, we should avoid trying to make others copy us. Relationships among members involve recognizing and bringing out the gifts and callings of others—not squelching their uniqueness to make copies of ourselves or to promote ourselves.

Because every believer has distinctive gifts, we are to interact appropriately with others but not attempt to duplicate someone else's gift. Some may think their gifts are less important and develop feelings of inferiority. But which member exhibits a particular gift is unimportant as long as the body is developing and maturing. God knows best how this should be done. As Paul wrote to Timothy, "In a large house there are articles not only of gold and silver, but also of wood and clay; some are for special purposes and some for common use" (2 Timothy 2:20).

While we must be careful to admire and respect those in spiritual leadership positions or who exercise certain high-profile gifts, we should never worship them. Rather, we should find contentment with the gifts God has placed in our own lives. If we seek the gifts of others for ourselves, it puts our will in a position of superiority over the will of God. There is a word for this: rebellion. If our self-centered desires were to be fulfilled, the body would become a sort of spiritual monster, with body parts out of proper proportion to one another.

At the other extreme, a member might feel his or her gifts are inferior to those of other believers. This also is poison for the body and should be avoided. Whatever our gifts and abilities, we should have sober judgment about them and provide humble service in the body of Christ, in accordance with the instruction given by Paul to the Church: "For by the grace given me I say to every one of you: Do not think of yourself more highly than you ought, but rather think of yourself with sober judgment, in accordance with the faith God has distributed to each of you" (Romans 12:3).

Just because there is a variety of different gifts doesn't mean we can pick and choose the ones we want. We are to use the innate qualities our Creator has given us for the good of the body. In his first letter to the Corinthians, Paul noted that "God has placed the parts in the body, every one of them, just as he wanted them to be" (1 Corinthians 12:18). Because of this divine order, we should appreciate that spiritual gifts are never to be used to advance ourselves as individuals or groups. They are more like common property, to be used for the benefit of the whole body.

The Benefits of Diversity

Diversity inside the body is an ingenious solution for volatility outside the body. Diversity is God's plan for us. It is not meant just to provide relief from boredom—like having dozens of different flavors of ice cream instead of merely one. It means many kinds of interaction become possible; these interactions are what make the body what it is. Diversity means we are more likely to have a solution on hand when innovation is needed. Diversity gives us a well-stocked toolbox so we can function as a living body.

There may not be another group of people as diverse as the body of Christ, since members represent all nationalities and cultural backgrounds. We have countless variations of gifts, personality traits, and points of view. Sometimes, when I meet believers from a background and culture different from mine, I sense that they are like me on a deeper level, which makes us kin. We can sense the kindred spirit we share: the Holy Spirit inside both of us. I wouldn't trust my own senses to be infallible all the time, but these encounters can and do occur.

Your body contains many different types of cells under one genetic code. It has unity amid diversity. Likewise, the body of Christ contains diverse members under one Lord. It has unity amid diversity. This combination makes for a healthy body. So, whatever you're good at, use those talents, gifts, and skills to benefit the body. If you don't offer your gifts to the body of Christ, they won't get contributed. Remember that you are unique. God made you for a reason—for the body of Christ.

QUESTIONS FOR DISCUSSION

1. Because spiritual unity is the structural essence of the body of Christ, we are intimately connected with every other living Christian in the world. How do you feel about the vulnerability of such close connections?

2. How would you contrast the promotion of conformity through rigid guidelines with the promotion of unity through vision and faith?

3. As believers, are we supposed to create unity or to maintain it? Explain.

4. Do you think the bonds among members of the body of Christ are stronger than bonds like nationality, social status, or religious denomination? Why?

5. Members cannot live if severed from the body; they will rot. A believer is not connected to the body of Christ as an individual but as a body member. How does this make you feel?

6. Where do our spiritual gifts come from? Do we obtain them through our own efforts? Why is it wrong to seek the gifts of others for ourselves?

7. The human body contains many different types of cells under one genetic code. It has unity within diversity. How does the body of Christ exhibit unity within diversity?

CHAPTER 10

ORDER IN THE BODY

But everything should be done in a fitting and orderly way.
—1 CORINTHIANS 14:40

I married my wife, Lydia, on the same day that the US-led allied forces launched a massive ground assault during the First Gulf War. As a result, my wife and I spent much of our honeymoon watching explosions and mayhem on CNN. That inspired one of our favorite humorous quips: "The war began the day we married."

With benefit of hindsight, our worries now seem a bit groundless. In that moment of history, though, we didn't know what would happen. We feared Saddam Hussein would launch chemical weapons against our troops—just one of numerous uncertainties and unknowns at the time. As in any war, despite our confidence in our military men and women, the final outcome could not be guaranteed.

Consider this:

- The Iraqi army outnumbered us.
- They had more bombs and bullets on hand.
- Not only were many of their soldiers battle proven by the protracted 1980s war with neighboring Iran, they were fighting to defend their families and homeland.
- They had plenty of time to entrench and build up defenses in anticipation of our invasion.

Yet despite being outmanned and outgunned, our tanks and other vehicles sped right through the heart of the enemy territory. Why such a lopsided victory for US-led forces in spite of the many disadvantages we faced? In his book *American Soldier*, General Tommy Franks explained:

> Going into Desert Storm, the Iraqi army had thousands of Soviet-built artillery pieces. They outgunned us by three to two. What doomed them was that they used those guns poorly. When their observation towers were destroyed and they lost their communications nets, they did not improvise and adapt . . . Our troops were a flexible, highly adaptable fighting force . . . The Iraqis had fielded more men, more tanks, and more artillery pieces than the Coalition. What defeated them was the combination of superior technology, realistic training, and the fluid, flexible tactics of the Coalition forces.[1]

As with many other autocratically governed organizations, the Iraqi army employed a traditional command-and-control structure. Because of that, troops on the ground received their commands from higher up. Not only did superior officers prohibit adaptation and self-determination, they severely punished it. When the US-led coalition destroyed their communication towers, the Iraqis did as they were trained to do: they hunkered down and awaited further orders. Following their training, they did not act on their own.

The coalition forces had been trained to act differently. The small, functional groups on the ground had been prepared and drilled, followed a defined mission, and possessed the necessary tools. Most importantly, *they had autonomy*. They could make decisions in real time as the situation changed. They were organized in a way similar to that of living bodies, which proved to be advantageous in battle.

THE BEAUTY OF ORDER

Order is another component of God's fingerprint on His creation. All living bodies are ordered on a variety of levels. The individual members coalesce into groups, and these groups function as building blocks for even larger groups.

Generally speaking, order comes about in living bodies when:

1. There are individual members.
2. The members have access to resources they need.
3. There is communication among members.

Like all other living bodies, the body of Christ has order and structure. So it follows there must be some sort of governance among its members. The writer of Hebrews said, "Have confidence in your leaders and submit to their authority, because they keep watch over you as those who must give an account. Do this so that their work will be a joy, not a burden, for that would be of no benefit to you" (Hebrews 13:17). But governance in a living body is unlike that often found in organizations, whether that be in business, systems of government, or traditional military commands. The conventional idea of hierarchical leadership places one person over another. In the body of Christ, though, each member is under the authority of the head, Christ. Those in positions of leadership must appreciate what the head is leading the members to do—not try to run things themselves or bark orders at underlings in an authoritarian style more suited to a dictatorship than to a living body.

PATTERNS OF PATTERNS

From a distance, we can admire the beauty of a snowy landscape, made up of countless bits of frozen water. Then, upon closer inspection, we can discern beautiful patterns of shapes in individual snowflakes. When we are able to inspect the tiny arms of each snowflake, another world of beauty opens up.

Similarly, we enjoy works of art because they delight us simultaneously on many levels. We are gratified not only by details of colors and shapes in a painting but also by how these elements interact on a larger scale. It's not just the melody, harmony, or progression of chords in a piece of music that tantalizes our senses; it's how everything works together at the same time. Beauty unfolds as the work is considered as a whole. There are different worlds of interaction as you go from a small scale to large scale. Our eyes and ears are constantly looking for patterns. When things are symmetrical and balanced and follow a pattern, we find beauty in them. When things are chaotic and follow no pattern, we see no beauty. God created us this way so that we will look for him in His creation. God leaves His fingerprint on creation. The patterns and common attributes across the world He has created show off aspects of His nature.

The beautiful patterns that exist across the works of God are present in His Church. Individuals interact to form small groups. These groups then interact in patterns, resembling the interactions among individuals. Then these smaller groups form larger groups that, in turn, interact in similar ways. The larger groups exhibit patterns of behavior based on the patterns found in the smaller groups and individuals from which they are built.

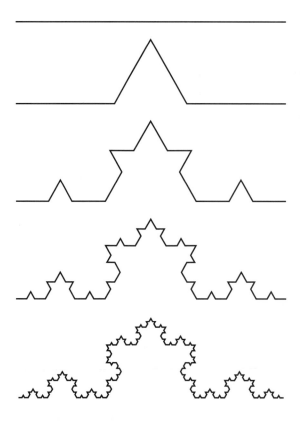

In fact, all living bodies have patterns of structure and patterns of activity recurring on different levels of scale. These build upon one another in turn. Consider the "patterns of patterns" seen in broccoli (fig. 1).

Fig. 1

The broccoli we see arises from a blueprint found in the genetic code—in the DNA of the plant. These genetic instructions for interactions among members are basic and straightforward. The members then become building blocks to create larger and larger structures. Patterns can be observed from the smallest to the largest components, because it is all based on the same simple set of genetic rules.

A fern leaf also has recurring patterns on many levels. When viewed as a whole, the leaf appears highly complex. However, on closer inspection, we can detect that only a few basic patterns are repeated over levels of scale. The Creator uses just a few simple instructions to fashion it. Because these instructions are applied on multiple levels, though, the leaf appears highly complex.

Even though the genetic code in DNA holds a large amount of data for the structure of the body, it cannot enter instructions for every interaction between every member. The simplicity of the way DNA works is ingenious. It provides basic instructions for each member. Members don't just follow dictates; rather, they apply these instructions to various circumstances. This is how a complex organism "emerges" from a simple set of instructions. DNA does not command; it furnishes instructions. It is a reference for cells to employ as they work out the details for their unique situations.

I think this is why we enjoy activities like checkers, basketball, or Monopoly. Games like this are based on a few simple rules or patterns of play, with the players free to make decisions along the way within those rules. Over time, each game plays out in ways that are not always predictable or expected; the pattern becomes more complex. The way the games work imitates the way God creates living beings. And when we play, we are subconsciously in tune with the way God creates living things.

THE BIBLE IS OUR GENETIC CODE

In the body of Christ, the Bible functions like the genetic code of a living organism. It does not provide exact details and commands concerning what actions we should take in every possible scenario. God's ingenious plan is giving us basic rules along with the liberty to make decisions based on those rules in different circumstances. For instance, we have the Ten Commandments, the "Golden Rule" (as Jesus said in Matthew 7:12: "So in everything, do to others what you would have them do to you, for this sums up the Law and the Prophets"), and other straightforward biblical rules for living. We apply these in the unique situations of our lives. So, even though there is nothing in the Bible about the internet, jet planes, or the United States, we can know how to interact with people in modern-day situations. We use the guidelines found in the Bible and live our lives according to Scripture, although the details are not necessarily dictated within its pages.

As believers live their lives based on instructions from the Bible, they gather together and become building blocks for even larger groups in the body. This creates the aforementioned "patterns of patterns" that allow the flexible and complex behavior of the body as a whole to emerge from rather simple rules. This is what happens with the instructions found in DNA in a physical body. In addition, it is what happens with the instructions found in the Bible when followed in the body of Christ.

The beauty of living bodies is found in their design. However, throughout the history of medicine, far too many physicians have viewed living bodies from a cold, impersonal, reductionist point of view. We dissect things down to their constituent elements in order to study the details and too often miss the artful way God has designed them.

THE ER

This is especially true in a hectic, mad-paced emergency room. Time seems to stand still against the backdrop of life-and-death situations. It feels like living in another dimension, where different rules and norms are in effect. Modesty is not recognized (personnel often rip clothes off the body of a trauma victim or cut them away). Individuality is lost, too, with patients treated as if they are essentially identical machines birthed from the same cosmic assembly line. Protocols often substitute for human reasoning or feelings. Death is seen as a natural part of life—not as some surreal or foreign event. Perception of the pain and agony of others becomes cold and objective (after all, you can't compromise your rationality by getting bogged down in the subjective). Saving a life is the goal, and that end justifies almost any means, no matter how distasteful those means seem to be to an outside observer. But by focusing on individual details, ER personnel can easily miss the wonder and beauty of the living body.

Our bodies are created in an artful way. Just as a painting inspires us or a symphony communicates with us on many levels simultaneously, the living body has many levels of order and beauty. With the aid of a microscope, the geneticist studies the intricate structures of chromosomes within nerve cells. The pathologist sees the marvel of these functioning cells on a higher level. The neurologist appreciates the orchestrated activities that groups of these cells exhibit on an even higher level. And the family doctor studies an even more intricate level of functioning as she interviews the patient in her office. All of these observers can find beauty if they take time to look beyond isolated parts.

So it is with the body of Christ. All over the world, believers acting on their own accord come together to form functioning groups. Over time, these groups coalesce into even larger entities. There are layers of associations in the living body of Christ. Individuals relate to one another; groups of individuals relate to other groups; and smaller groups unite to form larger groups. On each level, patterns reappear as individuals and groups structure themselves and relate to one another.

Remember how broccoli is designed with recurring patterns over different levels of scale? The way component parts of the body of Christ are put together and work, from the individual members to the whole body, also shows beauty in the design over different levels of scale. Yet members may not be able to take in this beauty if they live out their lives with a limited perspective. They must rely on the mind of Christ—namely, God's eternal point of view, which allows us to live on a much richer level of being.

In living bodies, the countless small activities of the members coalesce over time to form the large-scale activities of the organism. How things are done on the lower levels influences the overall body. Patterns on lower levels combine to form larger patterns. The ways members interact locally become the building blocks for larger activities in the body. Complexity increases as we move up the scale to higher levels. Each level builds on, and relies on, the patterns originating on the levels below it.

"Something Extra"

Good things occur spontaneously when the members of a body experience healthy relationships. Blessings materialize, and the whole becomes greater than the sum of the parts. This is called "emergence." Although

I mentioned Aristotle's "the whole is greater than the sum of the parts" outlook in chapter 1, it merits repeating here, listed as a mathematical equation:

Whole > [sum of the parts]

An equivalent way to write this:

Whole = [sum of the parts] + "something extra"

This "something extra" is what I mean by emergence. It represents the good things that emerge, both in everyday life and on a spiritual level in the body of Christ. This emergence is all around us on a daily basis—an example of hiding in plain sight. The whole becomes greater than the sum of the component parts. A few examples:

1. **Flocks of Birds Have No Clear Leader**
    The harmonized actions of a flock develop from unseen interactions among individual birds. You cannot predict flock behavior by studying the birds apart from one another. It is the "something extra" that emerges when individuals in the flock are in right relationship with one another and follow the straightforward rules of behavior given to them. However, if relationships among the birds are not right, the "something extra" does not emerge, and flock behavior does not come forth.

    In their leadership book *Lead Like Butler*, authors Kent Millard and Judith Cebula chronicled the extensive studies wildlife scientists have conducted to determine why geese and other migratory birds fly in a distinctive V formation. The scientists discovered that when geese fly together, each goose provides lift and reduces air resistance for members trailing behind, which means the whole flock can travel 70 percent farther with the same amount of energy than if each one flies alone. Not surprisingly, when a member drops out of the formation, it discovers it requires more effort and energy to fly. Geese help each other, too; if a goose is ill, shot, or injured, two others will fall out of formation to aid the injured member. They will remain with it and protect it from predators until it can fly again or dies. According to the authors, "Likewise, human teams work best when they do more than just work together, but care for the well-being of each other."[2]

2. A Composition Is More Than Its Notes

If you study the individual notes of a Beethoven sonata, they seem to be nothing more than random sounds. But when each note is placed in right relationship with the other notes, something greater materializes, and beautiful music unfolds. The beauty of a musical composition is the "something extra" that is more than the sum of the individual parts. If the notes are not in right relationship with one another, then there is no music, only noise. Imagine an orchestra with each member playing a favorite song without regard for what others are playing. The beauty of music would not emerge.

3. Capitalism Parallels Characteristics Found in Living Organisms

In capitalism, the "something extra" emerges from voluntary exchanges among people in the marketplace. Capitalism allows individuals freedom to interact autonomously, so a growing economy emerges out of their interactions, which is another "something extra" bonus. State-run economies often restrict this freedom of interaction. Their overall economy tends to be weaker because overregulation hinders relationships between individuals. No matter how noble or well intentioned, this stifling atmosphere does not allow the "something extra" to emerge.

Scholar Robert Murphy notes the issues with government- and society-run economies:

> This view is flawed in two major respects. First, it is impossible for a central authority to plan an economy. New technologies (if entrepreneurs have freedom to

create new technologies), changes in consumer taste (if consumers have freedom to pursue their tastes), and innumerable variables that can affect production, distribution, and consumption of everything from newspapers to lawnmowers on national or international scale are simply not "manageable" in the way socialist planners like to think they are. Second, the planning bias completely misunderstands the role of profit and loss in a market economy. Far from being arbitrary, a company's "bottom line" indicates whether an entrepreneur is doing what makes sense: if his product is one that people want and if he is using his resources in the best possible way.[3]

"Something extra" emerges when participants in an economy are allowed to freely buy and sell.

In the same way that economies, compositions, and flocks of birds can be greater than the sum of their parts, when connections among believers are healthy, we can experience the presence of Christ. Instead of only people being present, the Spirit of Christ joins us and creates something far greater than the humans involved. As Jesus told His disciples, "For where two or three gather in my name, there am I with them" (Matthew 18:20). The corollary to this is that when our relationships are not aligned in proper, biblically based order, then the presence of Christ is lacking. As James put it, "But if you harbor bitter envy and selfish ambition in your hearts, do not boast about it or deny the truth. Such 'wisdom' does not come down from heaven but is earthly, unspiritual, demonic. For where you have envy and selfish ambition, there you find disorder and every evil practice" (James 3:14–16).

LIFE AND DEATH

God has a way of encouraging believers to join with the body of Christ and live in communion with His Holy Spirit. As much as some of us may dislike the fact, or do our best to fight it with Botox and wrinkle-removing creams, or embrace cryogenic preservation in hopes that humans can achieve immortality (on earth) during the coming century, our bodies will eventually die and return to dust. All living things face death. Life is a cycle of new members being born to replace the old. God spelled this out when He delineated the consequences of Adam and Eve's disobedience, saying, "Cursed is the ground because of you; through painful toil you will eat food from it all the days of your life. It will produce thorns and thistles for you, and you will eat the plants of the field. By the sweat of your brow you will eat your food until you return to the ground, since from it you were taken; *for dust you are and to dust you will return*" (Genesis 3:19, emphasis added).

Just as God designed, cells in living bodies are continually dying and being replaced through the normal process of cellular growth and reproduction. To remain alive, living organisms use their resources to replace dying cells. This cycle of life and death is part of the natural order of our existence, even though we often want to ignore the inevitability of the latter.

Like many others who work in emergency rooms, I am well acquainted with the end of life. No job in the ER is more difficult than telling a family that their young son or daughter has died. As you might imagine, I have always disliked that aspect of my work. Still, being present at the moment of death many times has forced me to consider my own life in relationship to eternity. Hopefully, this has helped me shed delusions so I can be more truthful and honest about death.

The cyclical nature of life is underscored by the fact that we are born into this world and eventually die, with our physical bodies returning to the dust. Our human bodies are mortal, but God made us this way as a means of gently reminding us that the world is not our home. This is one way He has of coaxing us into the body of Christ.

QUESTIONS FOR DISCUSSION

1. In the Persian Gulf War, when the organic, US-led coalition destroyed their communication towers, the more traditionally organized Iraqis did as they were trained to do: hunker down and await orders. They were subsequently defeated. Consider this. What is the difference between the way organizations and living organisms operate?

2. Works of art can be found to have beauty on many levels of scale, from the smallest of details to the overall work. How is this similar to the way living bodies are designed? The body of Christ?

3. As illustrated in this chapter's broccoli example, "patterns of patterns" emerge in living things as we go from small scale to large scale. How does this resemble the way the body of Christ is designed?

4. God's ingenious plan is giving us basic instructions and the liberty to make decisions based on those instructions. How are the rules of a game such as checkers or Monopoly similar to the way the genetic code works? How are these rules like the Bible?

5. Jesus told His disciples, "For where two or three gather in my name, there am I with them" (Matthew 18:20). How do you feel about this promise? How have you seen it in action?

6. You cannot predict the behavior of a flock by studying individual birds. Flock behavior is the "something extra" that emerges when individuals in the flock are in appropriate relationship with one another and follow the straightforward rules of behavior given to them. What do you think we can learn from the way birds operate as a flock?

7. Imagine an orchestra with each member playing a favorite song without regard for what others are playing. What would the music sound like? What should members of the body of Christ learn from this?

CHAPTER
11

IMMUNE DISORDERS

Doctrines that biblically define salvation, Christ's deity and bodily resurrection, His virgin birth, and the infallible authority of Scripture are all nonnegotiables; they are central to our faith.[1]

—CORNERSTONE UNIVERSITY PRESIDENT JOSEPH STOWELL

I can remember it as if it happened last week. I was a newly graduated medical student in the first days of my practice. One sunny afternoon in the clinic, I felt a tingling sensation in both pinky fingers. These feelings increased over time. I then noticed weakness in my legs and feet; that evening, I grew concerned enough to invite my friends in a Bible study to pray for me. Early the next morning, I got out of bed for a shower and could not sense whether the water was hot or cold. While making my hospital patient rounds, I had difficulty walking unassisted. I even had to touch the wall with my hand to keep from falling over. Later that morning, I went to see a friend of mine who was an internist and was diagnosed with Guillain–Barré syndrome (GBS).

GBS is an immune system problem involving an attack on the nerve cells. The disease attacks the nerves in much the same way the immune system fights off an invading virus or an infection caused by something like a splinter in your finger. As a result, nerves become damaged and unable to function. Instead of carrying messages from the brain to the body, they can't do their work. So, the brain and body stop communicating with each other, which leads to paralysis. In spite of the brain remaining able to think and function, with no movement, normal life is no longer possible.

My neurologist admitted me to the ICU in anticipation of my impending quadriplegia. Over several weeks, the disease progressed to the point that I was completely incapacitated. During the next several months, a number of well-intentioned friends visited and did their best to comfort me in my time of need. Yet sometimes these visitations felt like an attack—particularly during attempts to uncover the "hidden" sins in my life that had brought on my illness. Just by looking at my situation, they thought it was obvious that I must have done something terribly wrong.

I could do little but lie there and listen, marveling over the same thing happening simultaneously on physical and spiritual levels. GBS was causing members of my body to attack other members because the disease had fooled them into not recognizing they were part of the same body. On another level, other believers were attacking me without understanding I was a member of the same body.

UNCOMFORTABLY NUMB

When I had GBS, it not only caused me to be unable to move but also made me unable to feel things normally. I was uncomfortably numb and in constant pain.

My visitors saw how devastating my paralysis was. But the numbness was just as overwhelming from my point of view. It's just that others couldn't see that part of the illness.

Both the paralysis and the numbness came about because parts of my body attacked and destroyed each other. When we attack one another in the body of Christ, it not only hinders our ability to move and interact in our world; it also shuts down our ability to feel. We no longer sense what is real around us. We lose perspective. We lose touch. And this can be just as devastating as the inability to function.

"SELF" OR "NOT SELF"?

GBS illustrates the incredible value of a properly balanced and functioning immune system. A healthy immune system stands guard against diseases by recognizing what is foreign to the body and what is not. In other words, it discriminates between what is "self" and what is "not self." It attacks things that are "not self" and leaves alone things that are "self." Immune systems function in many living animals. Even some plants have a rudimentary immune system, which means they are able to distinguish between themselves and other plants of the same species. Scientific experiments show that these plants grow roots that are fewer and shorter when close to roots of the same plant. Thus, they conserve valuable resources by not competing with themselves. They grow aggressively, though, when close to the roots of other plants.[2]

Having a functioning immune system is practical for good health. For example, if you get a splinter in your finger, your immune system recognizes it as a foreign object and attacks the splinter to flush it away. White blood cells come to the site and form pus, putting pressure on the splinter in a natural effort to expel it from the body. If an infecting virus or bacteria enters your body, the immune system recognizes it as an invader and mounts a response to get rid of it. At the same time, a healthy immune system recognizes the members of your body—such as heart cells, kidney cells, or skin cells—as part of the "self" and therefore does not attack them.

Problems with the immune system generally involve discrimination that is either too weak or too strong. This causes errors in recognizing what is meant to be part of the body and what is not. Individuals suffering from acquired immune deficiency syndrome (AIDS), a condition brought about by the human immunodeficiency virus (popularly known as HIV), have weakened immune systems that cannot discriminate well. AIDS causes the immune system to become tolerant of foreign invaders and fail to judge them as "not self." Because of this crippling condition, invading diseases are allowed to run rampant throughout the body and kill it.

As I mentioned in chapter 8, I was just starting my medical career in the early 1980s when medical researchers first identified AIDS. Since the treatments we offered then were not as advanced as they are today, many people rapidly succumbed to this devastating disease. I saw them die horrible deaths with all sorts of exotic infections because of weakened immune systems that could not distinguish between invaders and normal body parts.

Individuals with overly sensitive, aggressive immune systems may suffer from diseases at the other extreme of the spectrum, such as the GBS that temporarily sidelined me, as well as conditions like rheumatoid arthritis, lupus, and Graves' disease. In these conditions, the body has become too quick to decide that any one thing is "not self." The body begins attacking some of its own members, convinced they are foreign. In severe cases, these conditions can kill the body.

SPIRITUAL IMMUNE SYSTEM

A person becomes part of the body of Christ through rebirth, not through understanding.

But to be healthy, members of the body of Christ must know truth in order for their spiritual immune system to function. They must be able to discriminate between what is "self" and what is "not self." Without such a biblically grounded defense system in place, painful disabilities can afflict the body of Christ.

Legendary apologist Francis Schaeffer once noted:

> We must both distinguish true Christians from all pretenders and be sure that we leave no true Christians outside of our consideration. In other words, mere humanists and liberal theologians who continue to use the Christian label or mere church members whose Christian designation is only a formality are not to be accounted true. But we must be careful of the opposite error. We must include everyone who stands in the historic-biblical faith whether or not he is a member of our own party or our own group. But even if a man is not among the true Christians, we still have the responsibility to love him as our neighbor.[3]

When we have too little tolerance for other members of the body, we may be inclined to attack them and cause unnecessary division and harm. This is something like the physical devastation caused by an overactive immune system in GBS, rheumatoid arthritis, lupus, and Graves' disease.

Scripture emphasizes the importance of recognizing other members in Christ. As John wrote in his first epistle: "If anyone acknowledges that Jesus is the Son of God, God lives in them and they in God. And so we know and rely on the love God has for us. God is love. Whoever lives in love lives in God, and God in him" (1 John 4:15–16).

Soon after a contentious discussion with the Pharisees that inspired some of His detractors to pick up rocks in hopes of stoning Him, Jesus and His disciples passed by a blind man. That prompted the disciples to ask, "Rabbi, who sinned, this man or his parents, that he was born blind?" (John 9:2). They wanted to attack. Their question demonstrates how the disciples wanted to implicate someone for the blind man's condition. They wanted to know whether the man or his parents had sinned so they could assess blame. They were focused more on who had caused the problem than on helping someone in need.

Because human nature remains essentially the same two thousand years later, we too have an impulse to blame sick people for their illnesses, as evidenced by those who visited me during my bout with GBS. While it is true that some diseases result from self-inflicted behavior—such as overeating, alcohol abuse, or drug addiction—passing judgment on other believers causes the body of Christ pain and disability. This is especially true in instances of unforgiveness, which is why Paul advised the church at Ephesus: "Make every effort to keep the unity of the Spirit through the bond of peace" (Ephesians 4:3).

DIVIDE AND CONQUER

As I mentioned earlier, "church growth" is a term used to describe increases in attendance at church services. However, this too often means merely shuffling people in from other churches. We do so by managing things as a well-run business does, providing programs and services that attract consumers. Not only is this a tragic diversion from authentic discipleship, but it can promote a mind-set of competition in the body of Christ. When we contend with one another, we become distracted from recognizing Satan as our true enemy. Nothing is more destructive for the body than having one member or group of members attack others. When we are divided, we are conquered.

Scripture calls upon us to preserve the unity of the body. Our fight is not with other churches, denominations, or believers. It is with Satan and the anti-Christ worldview so pervasive in the modern world. If we do not recognize this, then we—as Paul wrote—are like one body part declaring it has no need of another: "As it is, there are many parts, but one body. The eye cannot say to the hand, 'I don't need you!' And the head cannot say to the feet, 'I don't need you!'" (1 Corinthians 12:20–21).

This appreciation for the body and the necessity of all its parts can help us gain a broader perspective on the eternal spiritual war we face. As in any war, it is imperative to understand who the enemy is, who we are, and our objectives. When it comes to the identity of our true enemy, it is not other believers. Have you seen a church or Christian organization where believers attack other believers and cause division? A friend of mine experienced a controversy in his old church about men's neckties. Some thought it was disrespectful for men to attend services without one. Others thought it was too showy for men to wear ties. Tragically, the church divided and ultimately dissolved over this petty issue.

Such fighting and division directly contradicts biblical advice about quarreling over nonessential issues:

> Who are you to judge someone else's servant? To their own master, servants stand or fall. And they will stand, for the Lord is able to make them stand. One person considers one day more sacred than another; another considers every day alike. Each of them should be fully convinced in their own mind. Whoever regards one day as special does so to the Lord. Whoever eats meat does so to the Lord, for they give thanks to God; and whoever abstains does so to the Lord and gives thanks to God. For none of us lives for ourselves alone, and none of us dies for ourselves alone. (Romans 14:4–7)

The Bible contains many other warnings about attacks and divisions among members of the body:

- "I appeal to you, brothers and sisters, in the name of our Lord Jesus Christ, that all of you agree with one another in what you say and that there be no divisions among you, but that you be perfectly united in mind and thought" (1 Corinthians 1:10).
- "I urge you, brothers and sisters, to watch out for those who cause divisions and put obstacles in your way that are contrary to the teaching you have learned. Keep away from them" (Romans 16:17).
- "If you bite and devour each other, watch out or you will be destroyed by each other" (Galatians 5:15).
- "Bear with each other and forgive one another if any of you has a grievance against someone. Forgive as the Lord forgave you" (Colossians 3:13).

LACK OF FORGIVENESS

When members attack one another and sow division, it inflicts pain and disability in the body of Christ. Often, the underlying cause is lack of forgiveness. In order to heal immune diseases in the body of Christ, we must forgive other members of the body and heal the divisions. If we fail to do so, we not only injure them but cut ourselves off from Christ. Jesus warned in His legendary Sermon on the Mount: "For if you forgive other people when they sin against you, your heavenly Father will also forgive you. But if you do not forgive others their sins, your Father will not forgive your sins" (Matthew 6:14–15).

Because we perceive reality through the distorted lens of our prior experiences, we see things, as Paul termed in 1 Corinthians 13:12, through a "glass, darkly" (KJV)—meaning with a poor reflection. So, Christ as the head, rather than we as members, ultimately determines membership in the body, as Paul wrote: "And he is the head of the body, the church; he is the beginning and the firstborn from among the dead, so that in everything he might have the supremacy" (Colossians 1:18).

DEBILITATING ATTACKS

Anyone who has been attacked by fellow church members or others in the body of Christ knows how debilitating such attacks can be. Despite the wounds inflicted on me as I lay in my hospital bed and listened to what sounded like inquisitions regarding my "secret sins," I was determined to find meaning in my situation. I had endured years of difficult training and given up time with family, friends, and pleasures in life in order to become a physician. Then, no sooner had I entered the medical field than GBS struck me down, leaving me unable to do anything for anyone. It seemed that all the time, effort, and considerable expense had been wasted. I wanted to know what the meaning of all of it was. I would lie in bed at night, with my mind alert but my body paralyzed, and cry out to God to give me some reason for it all. I found myself repeatedly asking Him, "Why?"

Then, around three o'clock one morning, I felt God's presence invade my hospital room. His peace overwhelmed me. I sensed Him communicating with me—mind to mind and Spirit to spirit. It wasn't an answer to the "Why?" question I had been asking. It was a response to the question I should have been asking instead. He said, "I am faithful." As soon as He said it, I knew the question that I should have concerned myself with was: "God, are You faithful?" At that point, I realized He is always faithful in every situation. He would take care of things. I did not have to find the meaning for my disease or the reasons for attacks from well-meaning visitors. I just needed to trust God.

The spiritual peace that engulfed me in those predawn hours reminded me of the most pleasant physical sensation I have ever experienced—when my wall of pain lifted. This happened one day in intensive care, and although it happened fairly quickly, in my muddled state of mind I wasn't sure if it took several minutes or several hours. Nor am I certain of whether God was answering my prayers to relieve the suffering or whether my nerves of sensation were just finally giving out after such a long battle. Whatever it was, the absence of pain felt exhilarating. This relief, combined with my body numbness, gave me the sensation of floating in midair. For a moment, I was on cloud nine, even though at the time I had little hope of resuming a normal life—and wasn't even sure I would survive.

One day, a young medical resident came to examine me in the hospital. He had no idea I was also a medical resident. Partway through the neurological exam, he looked at my chart and then back at me before tearfully exclaiming, "You're just like me!" Both completing our medical residencies at the time, we realized there was not that much difference between physician and patient. In the same way, there isn't that much difference between the clergy and lay members of a church. We are all part of the same body and fighting the same spiritual enemy. It helps to remember what we have in common with other believers.

ADOPTING A NEW VIEW

When it came to battling through GBS, the numbness seemed just as devastating as the paralysis. For quite a while, I could still wiggle my feet but had no sensation. No feeling, that is, except for the generalized pain constantly coming at me from all directions—without any discernible correlation with my physical body. Over time, this loss of sensation subtly changed the way I thought about myself. The severed communication link between my brain's impulses and my body completely destroyed my former self-view. (Over the years, we all develop a self-view. Mine had developed so inconspicuously that I had not even considered I had one.)

My body seemed separate from self, as if it were just another object in the environment. The hospital bed to which I was confined seemed as much a part of myself as my physical body. Although I understand humans to be triune beings composed of body, mind, and spirit, during my illness I had no use for my body. It struck me as excess baggage, because the daily work of the nursing staff and of hygiene, nourishment, and other tasks left me fatigued and more deeply in despair. And while my mind was alert for short periods of time, I spent most of my time sleeping. It was only my spirit that remained a vital part of me.

My recovery was not immediate. It took several months. Over time, though, I'm happy to say that the Lord did heal me and raise me up from my sickbed. Any time we endure an extended period of suffering, a financial shortage, or other woes, it is hard to praise God. But there is a bright side. According to the writer of Hebrews, "No discipline seems pleasant at the time, but painful. Later on, however, it produces a harvest of righteousness and peace for those who have been trained by it" (Hebrews 12:11).

Looking back, I can rejoice over the valuable lessons I learned—especially as a doctor. Some are critical of gruff physicians who lack a pleasant bedside manner. But my insights went much deeper than seeing the need for cordiality. I gained an intimate, personal view of how being a patient in our medical system can be dehumanizing. When I was sick, I felt like less of a person, as if I had dropped out of society. I was helpless, too—completely dependent on others for everything. Not only did I learn about the significance of compassionate nursing care, but I grew to appreciate the importance of human touch in our interactions.

I look at this painful experience as an education concerning the need for forgiveness in the body of Christ. Too often, slings and arrows characterize exchanges between Christians or among various denominations, networks, and parachurch organizations. Instead of drawing comfort and encouragement from other believers, we too often retreat into our "group," suspicious of all others, or embrace our particular interpretation of Scripture as the only valid one. When this happens, we allow our clever spiritual enemy to render us ineffective. When we stop attacking ourselves—like my overactive immune system that left me helpless for several months—we will be able to rise up and do the "greater things" that Jesus promised we would do.

QUESTIONS FOR DISCUSSION

1. Have you ever been sick or seriously injured, as the author was? How did visitors act when they came to see you?
2. In diseases such as GBS, an overly sensitive and aggressive immune system attacks other body parts as if they are not members of the body. How is this like unforgiveness in the body of Christ?

3. Nothing is more destructive for the body of Christ than one member attacking another. When we are divided, we are conquered. According to Ephesians 6:12, whom should we consider to be our enemy? Considering this, how should we act?

4. If you are in a large church, how do you feel about smaller churches? If you are in a small church, how do you feel about larger ones?

CHAPTER

12

The Dangers of Infection

Far from leading to an exodus, modern church growth
often uses the ideology and tools of Egypt to make the life
of the people of God more comfortable in captivity.[1]

—Author Os Guinness

It's been a while since Ebola became a household word in the United States, but at the time, I was amazed by how quickly the virus spread—along with the panic that touched our shores about a year after it surfaced in West Africa. A highly contagious and often fatal disease, Ebola virus disease causes fever, sore throat, muscular pain, and headaches, followed by vomiting, diarrhea, rash, and decreased functioning of the liver and kidneys. Before declared no longer an emergency in March of 2016, it sickened more than twenty-eight thousand West Africans and claimed more than eleven thousand lives.

Ebola came to America via missionaries flown here for treatment and via a Liberian tourist, who later died. The World Health Organization labeled it the worst outbreak of the virus in history.[2] Some thought it might even bring down the entire health-care system if things got too far out of hand. Before the Ebola scare erupted in this nation, we were not too discerning about it. It seemed far away and not much of a threat. Then the disease spread to a hospital near mine, partly because it was not on our radar yet. We did not see it coming because we had grown inattentive over time.

Yet, after the first case was discovered in the United States, we became quite discerning—almost overnight. Ebola spreads rapidly and is highly contagious. Working in the ER, we knew that when people got sick with the virus, the first place they would go would be the emergency room. That posed an immediate threat to those of us on the front lines. It was so contagious that if someone came in sick with Ebola, it would devastate the staff and create a domino effect. If enough of us got sick, it could shut down the entire health-care system.

We found ourselves having to think the unthinkable. As a result, we started donning outfits that resembled space suits to treat potential Ebola patients. We conducted Ebola drills and Ebola training. Anyone with a fever raised a "red flag," and we isolated that person for further screening. Out of an abundance of caution, we assumed anyone who came through the door had the virus until proven otherwise. For several months, we remained on high alert. Circumstances enhanced our discernment and sharpened our radar.

Some of the ER staff members said they feared a true Ebola epidemic so much that if one started, they wouldn't be able to come to work. "If it comes down to treating Ebola patients in the emergency room, I'm calling in sick," one told me. "For the sake of my family, I just can't take that risk. If I get infected and get home and my kids get sick, they could die."

This was a very real possibility at the time. About a mile from the hospital where I worked, a forty-five-year-old man visiting the United States from Liberia showed up at another ER with a high fever and body aches—and was sent home after initial treatment. A day later, he returned, was admitted, and died a few days later from Ebola virus disease. Two nurses developed the illness from contact with him, despite wearing the same kind of "space suit" that our hospital used. Fortunately, they recovered, but as the news spread about their condition, the fears became uppermost in our minds. We questioned the effectiveness of our "PPE" (personal protective equipment) and whether it would truly keep us safe. While people in the health-care system want to do everything possible to protect our patients' lives, we don't want to needlessly sacrifice our own in the process.

The Ebola scare exposed the fragile nature of our health-care system. It was a very real possibility that the system—at least, the primary care aspect—could collapse. Fortunately, it didn't, but that isn't a guarantee that another threat won't arise to threaten it in the future.

DEADLY INFECTIONS

Infectious diseases—like Ebola and the Zika virus that caused some athletes to skip the 2016 Summer Olympics and pregnant women to amend their travel plans—generate international headlines. Less noticeable are the ways the "spirit of the age" can infect our thinking and worm its way into the church. It can be every bit as deadly as a virus and has the same potential—especially in an age of instantaneous, worldwide social media—to quickly spread throughout the body. Because it can be so devastating, we must constantly be on the lookout and ascertain when there is a risk to our spiritual health.

Nonbiblical viewpoints are continuously vying to gain a foothold in the body of Christ. They have ever since Jesus walked this earth, as evidenced by Paul's admonishment of the elders of the church at Ephesus: "Keep watch over yourselves and all the flock of which the Holy Spirit has made you overseers. Be shepherds of the church of God, which he bought with his own blood. I know that after I leave, savage wolves will come in among you and will not spare the flock. Even from your own number men will arise and distort the truth in order to draw away disciples after them" (Acts 20:28–30).

Indeed, throughout his ministry, Paul issued warnings to Christ's followers about the hazards of false doctrine:

- "See to it that no one takes you captive through hollow and deceptive philosophy, which depends on human tradition and the basic principles of this world rather than on Christ. For in Christ all the fullness of the Deity lives in bodily form, and you have been given fullness in Christ, who is the head over every power and authority" (Colossians 2:8–10).
- "I am astonished that you are so quickly deserting the one who called you to live in the grace of Christ and are turning to a different gospel" (Galatians 1:6).

- "Since you died with Christ to the basic principles of this world, why, as though you still belonged to it, do you submit to its rules?" (Colossians 2:20)
- "Avoid godless chatter, because those who indulge in it will become more and more ungodly. Their teaching will spread like gangrene . . ." (2 Timothy 2:16–17).

Because of this, we must constantly use wisdom and exercise discernment to avoid succumbing to these infectious agents. Judge what people say and teach, using the Bible as your "gold standard." Do not accept false notions based on emotion or sentiment. Do not have the "itching ears" about which Paul warned his protégé, Timothy: "For the time will come when people will not put up with sound doctrine. Instead, to suit their own desires, they will gather around them a great number of teachers to say what their itching ears want to hear. They will turn their ears away from the truth and turn aside to myths" (2 Timothy 4:3–4).

Paul's instruction echoed what Jesus told His followers in the Sermon on the Mount: to be on guard against false prophets. "They come to you in sheep's clothing, but inwardly they are ferocious wolves" (Matthew 7:15).

When it comes to the body of Christ, infection spreads the same way it does in the physical body. It can be thought of as a process whereby foreign DNA invades, gains a foothold, grows, and then, over time, weakens and destroys the parts of the body with which it comes into contact. Spiritual infection may occasionally relate to doctrinal difficulties that arise. But the analogy of infection that I perceive as the most serious in the church is the gradual acceptance of worldly philosophies and practices, which is followed by an ensuing decline in effectiveness. At the bottom, the body of Christ assumes "room temperature," meaning it becomes one with its surrounding environment. In other words, it is a spiritual death.

THE DANGERS OF DECEPTION

False philosophies permeate our world. The Bible says to beware of anything that directs us in ways other than the truth that God has established. These philosophies are like wolves in sheep's clothing. Since they are so deceptive, many sound innocent on the surface. We are told that we should always be tolerant and loving or that while various faiths take a slightly different path, ultimately, they all lead to God. "After all, in the end, isn't the point the same? Can't we accept all faiths as truth?" people ask. While such statements may sound innocent, they aren't. They are like the "savage wolves" about which Paul warned the Ephesians. When Jesus told us to be careful of such wolves, He wasn't being intolerant or judgmental. He was being informative. God is truth, and anything contradictory to His truth is not Truth with a capital T.

We need discernment to guard against this because the world exerts a never-ending pressure on the church to accept its way of looking at issues. It doesn't matter whether it is the false god of materialism; the "everyone is going to heaven" outlook known as universalism; or the idea that if we just love everyone enough, we won't have any enemies. I read a story recently about the persecuted church in which a believer discussed how the church became an inevitable target of ISIS after civil war broke out in Syria in 2011. "In 2009 Syria was one of the 10 safest countries in the world," the author writes. "The secure environment has vanished from the whole nation because of the sectarian war between Shiites and Sunnis. We are the enemy of both sects. We began to see pressure from radicals who wanted to 'Islamicize' Syria and eradicate Christians and other minorities. Nobody wanted us. We tried to stay out of the fight but we couldn't."[3]

One should be careful about painting Muslims into an "us versus them" dichotomy. The conflicts between Shiite and Sunni Muslims are as bitter (if not more so) as radical Islamists' hatred of the United States. Still, the idea that Islam is a peace-loving religion flies in the face of the continuing worldwide attacks by jihadists who are all Muslims. Yet, on a national level, our leaders have embraced this very outlook. Soon after terrorists took down the World Trade Center in September 2001, President George Bush declared that the face of terror is not the true faith of Islam. Speaking at the Islamic Center in Washington, DC, Bush said, "That's not what Islam is all about. Islam is peace. These terrorists don't represent peace. They represent evil and war. When we think of Islam we think of a faith that brings comfort to a billion people around the world. Billions of people find comfort and solace and peace. And that's made brothers and sisters out of every race."[4]

Consequences Unfold

It's one thing for a president to mention this in a speech but another when it takes foot as official government policy. Fast-forward fifteen years, and we can see the outcome of pursuing this outlook, as exemplified by the federal "Countering Violent Extremism" (CVE) program that prohibits the FBI from factoring in the Islamic component in its investigations of terrorism. When FBI agents uncover clear evidence of such involvement, they are required to ignore it. What is patently obvious must be ignored; what is patently false must be accepted.

The consequences of this approach were on vivid display in December of 2015 when Syed Farook and Tashfeen Malik opened fire at an office building in San Bernardino, California, killing fourteen individuals and wounding twenty-two people who were attending a county health department training event and Christmas party. Hours later, after pursuing their vehicle, police killed the married couple in a shoot-out. Farook was an American-born US citizen of Pakistani descent, while his Pakistani wife was a lawful, permanent US resident. Despite everyone acknowledging the obvious, it took four days before former President Barack Obama declared the shooting an act of terrorism.

Less than two weeks after the tragedy, author Andrew McCarthy detailed for *National Review* how Malik had written social-media posts that endorsed jihad and expressed disdain for America, yet immigration agents didn't question (or deny) her admission to the United States. Indeed, according to McCarthy, the government consciously avoided it because of its CVE "antiterrorism" program. The author said that government officials conceded that Malik was inadequately screened before she was permitted to relocate to the United States on a K-1 (nonimmigrant) visa, issued because she was the fiancé of an American citizen.

McCarthy went on to describe how, despite Malik's active use of social media, government investigators didn't discover these posts until after the San Bernardino massacre. It is not enough to say that security and intelligence agencies missed signs of the Islamist mind-set, he wrote. The author explained the government *chose* to miss them:

> As a matter of policy, the Department of Homeland Security . . . avoids looking at, much less scrutinizing, the publicly available social-media commentary of aliens who seek visas to enter the United States, including from Islamic countries that are jihadist strongholds . . .
>
> The fact of the matter is that Tashfeen Malik was issued a visa not because of an insane "secret" visa policy, but because of the Obama administration's criminally irresponsible but quite public national 'security' strategy—'Countering Violent Extremism.' . . . In essence, CVE holds that terrorism has nothing to do with Islam, or even with Islamist ideology that reviles the United States. According to President Obama, "Muslim American communities have categorically condemned terrorism"—as if that were an incontestable proposition or one that told the whole story. Thus . . . the real threat to our security, [the CVE guidance instructs], is not Muslim terrorist plots against us but our provocation of Muslims by conveying the misimpression that America is at war with Islam.[5]

Among other shocking reports that followed this were several neighbors telling an ABC outlet in Los Angeles that while they had noticed suspicious activity at Farook's home and at his mother's at another location, they didn't say anything. Aaron Elswick, a neighbor of Farook's mother, had noticed "quite a few packages" arriving within a short period of time: "'They were actually doing a lot of work out in the garage,' he said, adding that the neighbor was 'kind of suspicious' and 'wanted to report it,' but 'didn't want to profile' Farook and his family."[6]

One columnist in the aftermath of this tragedy noted the parallels between this incident and the shooting of forty-two soldiers (thirteen of whom died) in 2009 in Fort Hood, Texas: "This is the same politically correct culture that led to the Ft. Hood shootings of when Nidal Hassan, who had been spouting violent Islamic propaganda to neighbors on post and reaching out to Al [sic] Qaeda, was ignored for fear of 'Islamaphobia' accusations. . . . See something, say something, is dead."[7]

Resisting Intimidation

Allowing people to intimidate us into silence can have fatal consequences in the world, but even more so in the body of Christ. For the past several decades, American society has been following a situational ethics philosophy, according to which black becomes white, right becomes wrong, and we struggle to label anything as "over the line" of morals and good taste. What's worse—in today's flood of social media, online content, and countless entertainment options and other alternatives competing for our attention—individuals are losing the ability to think critically. They either cannot tell the difference between fact and opinion, or else the difference doesn't matter to them.

This "dumbing down" of society can adversely affect our spiritual discernment. For any number of reasons, we are now expected to tolerate things that the Bible calls immoral or untrue. We know it, too. However, in recent times, this has moved even further, from mere tolerance to normalization. We once "tolerated" things we knew to be wrong to keep peace in society. Currently, we are expected to treat the immoral as moral and the false as true. This is beyond tolerance. It is the end of discernment.

If the body of Christ accepts the ways of the world as normal, we become ineffective and sick. When the ways of the world creep into how we as Christians think, we can become infected. If this happens and the body of Christ doesn't take steps to halt the spread of infection, it will be the end of our witness to the world.

We need to take action similar to the way the medical community treats Ebola. When the virus first became a threat, we learned that the only proven, effective method of treating patients with it was a blood transfusion. Doctors would take blood from a patient who had recovered from the virus and give it to someone suffering from the disease to furnish that person with a passive immunity, meaning one not generated by their own system.

Hopefully, we can prevent infection and, if it does occur, treat it using spiritual methods.

Prevention is based on the ability to determine right from wrong, which comes from knowing the Bible and its teachings. That doesn't mean memorizing a long list of verses but reading and studying it regularly and taking its lessons to heart. Fellowship with other followers of Christ and maintaining close relationships with them to provide accountability in our lives can also help us develop wisdom and recognize the difference between right and wrong. This is the reason being part of a local church is so important—not so that we can say we attended a weekend worship service but so that we can develop close relationships and be exposed to biblical instruction.

HEALING FROM WOUNDS

A time of healing is required after we contract an infection. We need to remember to show other believers love and welcome them into the body if they have been ravaged by unbiblical teachings or the ways of the world. I know a mother named Lisa whose husband became so swept up in the legalistic teaching of Old Testament law that it cost them their marriage. She chose to leave for her own safety, as well as for that of her children, commenting, "That religious spirit that has no compassion in it has scarred me for the rest of my life."

Throughout this ordeal, she has remained a member of the same church, a seeker-sensitive-type environment that sees several thousand people coming through its sanctuary every weekend. When she finally divorced her verbally and physically abusive husband, however, and faced her first Thanksgiving without any of her four children in her home, she felt alone and abandoned. A backslidden Christian whom she had met in the business world invited her to join him and his brother for dinner. They offered the kind of comfort, companionship, and solace she wishes she could have found in her own congregation.

"Week after week, on Sunday, people would say, 'How are you doing?'" Lisa recalls. "But nobody wanted to hear about the horrors I was going through day after day or about my ex-husband's rigid beliefs, which he tried to control me with. Climbing out of those situations was incredibly difficult. I never felt lower and more abandoned, and yet these people who didn't know the Lord embraced me and took me in. To this day, I love my pastor, but if I wasn't as deeply rooted in my faith as I was, I would have left."

Despite this disappointment with her church, her friendships with other Christians (including my wife, Lydia) helped her rebuild her life and heal from this traumatic experience. One friend spent two hours a day with her on the phone during the most painful period of her divorce proceedings, consoling her, listening to her, and helping prevent her from "losing her mind." Knowing people who realized all the complexities of her situation and who would pray for her without judging her proved to be a huge blessing.

Still, she says everyone in the church is so tied up that she feels we have equated "busyness" with "success." Lisa wishes more pastors would emphasize the message that only when we extend the spirit of love, compassion, and hospitality will we see a reversal in the decline of the modern church. She remarks that many Christians are so busy running their kids to sporting events, academic competitions, and other activities that they can never find time to offer hospitality to others in the spirit of 1 Peter 4:9.

"I think the church has lost that," Lisa observes. "After church, we should be asking ourselves, 'Who looks lost and could use help? Who can I reach out to?' Seeing someone you can invite over or have fellowship with would have done worlds of good in my case. A lot of people asked, 'How are you doing?' when they knew I was going through a divorce. It's critical to have a biblical community. The church is dying. I doubt my children will stay with it, even though they love church. Unless we get our act together, the body of Christ won't survive."

QUESTIONS FOR DISCUSSION

1. Nonbiblical points of view are continuously vying to gain a foothold in the body of Christ. How is the "spirit of the age" like an infecting germ for the body?

2. How is discernment helpful in preventing "infection" in the body of Christ?

3. Jesus told us to be careful of "ferocious wolves" in sheep's clothing (Matthew 7:15). Does this mean we should be tolerant of other views? How far should we take this?

4. We are to implement our critical thinking skills and exercise discernment. How does tolerance of immorality differ from normalization of immorality?

5. Cells in a living body are able to recognize infecting germs because they are acquainted with their genetic code. How does studying the Bible help us avoid infection in the body of Christ?

6. The Ebola virus has been successfully treated by employing blood transfusions from survivors of the disease. What parallels can you see for using the wisdom of mature saints in the body of Christ to bring about healing in a contentious situation?

CHAPTER

13

THE PARASITE KNOWN AS CANCER

*Some cells do choose to live in the body, sharing its
benefits while maintaining complete independence—
they become parasites or cancer cells.*[1]

—THE LATE DR. PAUL BRAND, HAND SURGEON

When I talk with patients about their medical problems and their desire
for healing, the subject of miracles often arises. I'm always cautious not
to raise false expectations. Still, I have seen miraculous healings take
place. During my childhood, it was not unusual to hear testimonies from
people who had been healed of all sorts of ailments. These impromptu
reports were frequently given in the "testimony service" phase of church
meetings. Some of these healings were likely psychosomatic or not
miraculous. Yet things happened that could not be explained through
scientific or natural means. As a boy, I saw the blind see and the deaf hear
after sessions of intense prayer.

Lydia and I are blessed to have come from families with rich traditions of prayer for the sick and Christian ministry. Lydia's family helped
start the *Voice of Healing* magazine, which documented people who were
healed through prayer in the great revival meetings of the 1940s. Her
mother was the magazine's first editor; the original printing equipment
was housed in their family garage.

So, it may not surprise you that I pray with my patients whenever
appropriate. Instead of being upset, most have expressed their appreciation for the prayer. In fact, I have asked thousands of patients over
the years if they would like prayer, and only one has declined. Indeed,

we make prayer an integral part of our medical practice. When my wife and I opened a medical practice in Arlington, Texas, we did not accept government or insurance payments because we wanted to maintain the freedom to pray with patients as we provided them with medical care.

One afternoon, a young man came into our clinic. After he paid for the visit, my administrator found him alone in the waiting room—in excruciating pain. Since I was busy with other patients, she took the initiative to pray with him. Immediately, his symptoms left. He told her he no longer needed to see me, so she refunded his money and he left, praising God! This kind of healing is certainly a blessing for the recipient but difficult to confirm scientifically. In fact, most miraculous healings are difficult to authenticate beyond a reasonable doubt. There are exceptions, though.

MIRACULOUS HEALING

I later had a patient named Gene. He came to me for an evaluation of a growing nodular mass on the front of his right thigh. A healthy individual, he didn't visit any doctor on a whim. Gene came to see us because this growth was steadily growing and interfering with normal daily life. A pinkish-purple color, it was several inches wide. I couldn't give him an immediate diagnosis, so I removed a piece of the tumor and sent it to our pathologist for evaluation. A few days later, my heart sank when the report returned: Merkel cell carcinoma, or MCC.

This is a serious form of skin cancer. It has to be treated with surgery to remove the tumor and lymph nodes—often in combination with chemotherapy or radiation therapy. If not treated aggressively early on, it can cause death. Many people die in spite of treatment. But without treatment, death is almost certain.

Like other forms of cancer, MCC occurs when previously normal cells have a mutation in the written code of their DNA that spurs unregulated growth. The cells multiply at a fierce rate and spread to surrounding tissues and regional lymph nodes. They can enter the blood stream, too, and travel to distant parts of the body to wreak havoc. Once the cells start down this path, they destroy other cells with which they come into contact.

I dreaded the day Gene returned to discuss his report. At his initial consultation, we had prayed for the Lord to give him health and to guide me in providing his medical care. Now, thanks to his deep faith in God, he wasn't anxious. Not even after I told him, "Gene, I'm afraid the report is bad. You have a serious form of skin cancer. You will need to see a surgeon right away to have the tumor and lymph nodes removed if you have any chance of surviving." Instead of getting upset, he asked if we could pray. Then I scheduled an appointment for him with a surgeon.

Gene came back to see me a few days later. He had been to see the surgeon, who had suggested a treatment plan that would include immediate surgery to remove the cancerous mass. Still, since Gene felt the Lord would heal him through prayer, he wanted to postpone any treatment until he had prayed further about the situation. I disagreed and told him I thought it would be a mistake to postpone surgery. After all, I told him, "There is nothing wrong with doing all you can do to help the situation while you pray."

Gene did not agree with my reasoning. He started a regimen of prayer and meditation several times each day. He did not accept any medical treatment. I was more than a little surprised to see the tumor shrinking instead of enlarging as expected. Over several months, it completely vanished!

This experience prompted me to write the following letter. (By the way, one reason more medical miracles aren't "documented" is so few doctors are willing to verify them. They fear either some kind of lawsuit or ridicule from their peers and skeptics who scoff at the idea of divine healing.)

To whom it may concern:

I am writing this letter with the permission of my patient.

Four months ago, I evaluated him in my office for a lesion on the surface of his right anterior thigh, which had been growing in size for some time. This lesion was biopsied and proved to be Merkel cell carcinoma (neuroendocrine carcinoma). This type of tumor has a poor prognosis if not treated aggressively early on, similar to what is seen with malignant melanoma.

We discussed treatment options at length. I felt that he should waste no time in having aggressive treatment. I strongly encouraged him to undergo a surgical procedure for removal of the local tumor and the lymph nodes in the groin, which may have been involved also.

My patient did see a surgeon to discuss this but became thoroughly convinced that he did not want any surgical intervention. His alternative to surgery was to pray several times a day for healing.

When I reexamined him, the tumor appeared to be completely gone. There was an indentation on the right thigh in the place where the tumor had been previously. I am led to believe he experienced remission of this cancerous tumor due to prayer and his faith in God. Consideration of the serious nature of this cancer, along with the lack of medical intervention obtained by him, leaves me no other conclusion.

—RON BRYCE, MD

PUTTING OTHERS FIRST

I share this story to emphasize that we serve a miracle-working God, who designed the body of Christ to be His hands, feet, and arms on this earth as we share the gospel and do good works.

As I am typing these words, I have bandages on several injured fingers. As you can imagine, that makes the act of typing a bit painful. If I imagine myself as one of those fingers in the body of Christ, I might be tempted to complain. After all, the finger is hurting. But that is only because the finger would not have a full-orbed vision for a higher purpose, like writing this book. The sore finger feels just the pain and wants to ask God, "Why are You allowing this to happen to me?"

To fail to grasp a higher purpose behind life's setbacks and to erupt with grumbling, moaning, and complaining are akin to cancer attacking the physical body. Cancer in the body occurs whenever a cell wants to follow its selfish desires and go its own way. Anyone who has suffered from cancer understands the pain and disability it causes. Think of how difficult it must be for the body of Christ to fulfill its mission on earth when members become self-serving and manipulative rather than charitable and honest. Likewise, to remain a nonmalignant part of the body of Christ requires us to go through difficulties and suffering at times. While looking to something higher than ourselves, we may need to give up some comforts of this world. We may even be required to suffer at times.

As we have seen amid increasing hostility to followers of Christ in various parts of the world, such a decision may even lead to martyrdom. Yet sometimes the suffering and sacrifice of one part of a body are necessary for the survival of the whole. Anyone who has seen *Saving Private Ryan* is familiar with heroic actions taken by soldiers to save their comrades in arms. Sometimes, those acts mean giving their lives so that others might live and so that the cause for which they are fighting can advance. This type of self-sacrifice may seem like madness to someone with a self-centered worldview. However, it is not madness when we reach decisions based on the knowledge that there is an entity higher than ourselves in the universe.

We must not look at temporary setbacks, pain, or changes as necessarily being evil; these things may be taking place as a benefit for the overall body. It is important that we see things from God's viewpoint as we are engaged in the activities of our day-to-day lives.

The truth is that, as the body of Christ, each of us is connected to others—regardless of country, denomination, or other affiliation. But do I see myself as part of this larger body or as an unattached individual? Do I understand there is a Higher Being at the center of my universe or take the cancerous position of placing myself at the center? When individuals, a local fellowship, or another group in the body of Christ emphasize their own growth, they are becoming independent of the headship of Christ.

SACRIFICING FOR THE WHOLE

Do you know people who selfishly seek personal pleasures and happiness as their number-one purpose in life, only to wind up growing bitter over time? Often, happiness escapes us if we chase after it as our goal. We can spend the bulk of our lives trying to advance our own interests as we reach for a place of comfort and personal satisfaction. But this kind of self-centered action is an apt description of how cancer originates. A part of the body frees itself from normal restraints and does not abide by the instructions in its genetic code. The result is unrestrained growth. It invades other parts of the body and chokes them off. With the other members dying, the ultimate paradox is that the cancerous part destroys itself by not functioning in submission.

The impact of rebellious, self-centered, self-seeking individuals can be as fatal to the church as this dreaded disease is on the physical body. The unsubmitted part can destroy a local church and inflict even more widespread damage as the person (or people) throws off restraint. Whenever we give priority to our personal comfort, selfish desires, and personal preferences—be it worship style, color of the carpet, or our opinion of the preacher's sermons—we become analogous to cancer in a physical body.

Striving to promote unity in the body and the betterment of the worldwide church reflects people who discover a goal higher than self-interest toward which to work. When they put that higher purpose above their own comfort and pleasure, happiness tends to follow. Ironically, we seldom achieve happiness when that is our primary objective. It comes only as a secondary benefit when we focus our vision on a higher calling.

Individual sacrifice is sometimes necessary for the good of the body. We should seek to spend our lives doing God's will, even when it does not seem to benefit us in the short term. Wholeness and health ultimately result when members of the body of Christ are passionate about Him, seek to advance His cause in the world, and love "not their lives even unto death" (Revelation 12:11 ESV).

Physicians use their skills to alleviate pain and suffering. Yet if that is our sole focus, patients may become progressively worse even though they might temporarily feel better. When we treat people with serious diseases, it is not acceptable to treat only the symptoms and not address the core issues causing their problems. A good physician looks not merely at immediate relief but also at the patient's future well-being. After all, I have yet to see a baby born who isn't brought into this world against his or her will. They always look as if they are being born against their better judgment.

Our model is our Lord and Savior. Jesus did not prevent Roman soldiers from arresting Him, even though He was so powerful that when He replied, "'I am he,' they drew back and fell to the ground" (John 18:6). He did not come off the cross and wipe out the Roman army, even though He easily could have and even though He was right and they were wrong. If He had done this, He would have been putting selfish interests ahead of the Father's plan. While it might have been the fair thing to do, Jesus was not concerned with fairness or with whether His rights had been infringed upon. Far more important things were at play. There are principles we are required to follow in spite of our rights or what seems fair—or how tough it is to see them through. Christ demonstrated that in the garden of Gethsemane. While he desperately wanted not to die a painful death on a criminal's cross, "He went away a second time and prayed, 'My Father, if it is not possible for this cup to be taken away unless I drink it, may your will be done'" (Matthew 26:42).

A WOODPECKER STORY

Mark Rutland, a respected leadership consultant and former president of Southeastern University and Oral Roberts University, shared the following story many years ago when he was on staff at a church in Atlanta. Once, a woodpecker flew to a limb of a tree on top of a hill. Just as he pulled his head back and began to peck, a mining crew working down below set off explosive charges that blew off the top of the hill. The explosion blasted the woodpecker off the tree. He landed half a mile away. After he came to his senses and shook the dust off his feathers, he crawled back home to his nest. His wife was there waiting on him for supper. He crawled up to her and said, "You'll never guess what I did today!"

Whenever God blesses us with a miracle, one of the problems is that we are tempted to take ownership and say, "Look what I did!" Yet I can't claim any more credit for the healing of my cancer patient, Gene, than the woodpecker could claim for that explosive charge. When you find yourself with a blessing or when God has performed a miracle of healing in your life, it's easy to fall prey to the thought that you did something special. Sometimes well-intentioned people want to help others receive the same miracle or blessing that they enjoyed. Often, the tendency is telling others to follow a certain method or do things a certain way if they want to experience a similar blessing or healing.

The difficulty with this kind of approach is it tends to puff us up and make us think we did something on our own, through our own efforts or abilities. When we do this, we lose charity as our motivating factor in the way we do things. The sometimes all-too-human methods that we teach can take on a life of their own. As Paul put it in his letter to the Galatians, "If anyone thinks they are something when they are not, they deceive themselves" (Galatians 6:3). He also wrote to the Corinthians, "For it is not the one who commends himself who is approved, but the one whom the Lord commends" (2 Corinthians 10:18).

Ministries and churches built on the personality of a strong leader may be tempted to go down the path of self-aggrandizement and human-centered appeals. We should be careful to put our hope not in a person but in Jesus Christ and to follow biblical teachings with humility and charity. By ignoring biblical guidelines and living our lives looking out primarily for our own interests, we are behaving like cancerous cells. However, when we live charitably, doing the will of the Lord even when it does not benefit us in the short term, we can experience wholeness and health.

Have you who have served in a church or Christian ministry ever run across believers who seemed "puffed up" and self-serving? Paul explained that we can be the greatest individual possible, but without love (charity), this means nothing: "If I speak in the tongues of men or of angels, but do not have love, I am only a resounding gong or a clanging cymbal. If I have the gift of prophecy and can fathom all mysteries and all knowledge, and if I have a faith that can move mountains, but do not have love, I am nothing. If I give all I possess to the poor and give over my body to hardship that I may boast, but do not have love, I gain nothing" (1 Corinthians 13:1–3).

CANCER PREVENTION

I love 1 Corinthians 13, which I think contains the perfect prescription for the prevention of cancer in the body of Christ. The Creator designed love as the way to avoid the self-consuming, self-centered, self-destroying aspects of human nature that can run amok in the body of Christ. It is much better to avoid cancer before it starts than to deal with the serious consequences of treatment.

I know this as a result of treating so many of my patients who have suffered from cancer. Some say they would rather die than simply prolong the agony and endure the nausea, fatigue, hair loss, and overwhelming infections allowed by an immune system weakened by the treatments. Then there is the financial strain that accompanies the inability to work and the copays and uncovered medical expenses. Others give up when their life turns into a never-ending series of doctor visits, chemotherapy and radiation treatments, lab tests, body scans, and other medical appointments.

In the same way unpleasant symptoms accompany cancer treatment, correcting problems in the body of Christ can also be very unpleasant. Still, when a member of the body does not follow the "love chapter," becomes puffed up, and leads others astray, that member must be lovingly confronted. The guidelines that Jesus spelled out in Matthew are quite strict: "If your brother or sister sins, go and point out their fault, just between the two of you. If they listen to you, you have won them over.

But if they will not listen, take one or two others along, so that 'every matter may be established by the testimony of two or three witnesses.' If they still refuse to listen, tell it to the church; and if they refuse to listen even to the church, treat them as you would a pagan or a tax collector" (Matthew 18:15–17).

When we are forced to confront uncharitable members of the body of Christ, our goal is not to punish, win a debate, or demonstrate our superior biblical knowledge but to guide the person back to the ways of Christ. This is the point at which another portion of Paul's words from 1 Corinthians 13 is so appropriate: "Love is patient, love is kind. It does not envy, it does not boast, it is not proud. It does not dishonor others, it is not self-seeking, it is not easily angered, it keeps no record of wrongs. Love does not delight in evil but rejoices with the truth. It always protects, always trusts, always hopes, always perseveres" (4–7).

Matthew relates a time when Jesus spoke of the supremacy of love: "Hearing that Jesus had silenced the Sadducees, the Pharisees got together. One of them, an expert in the law, tested him with this question: 'Teacher, which is the greatest commandment in the Law?' Jesus replied: 'Love the Lord your God with all your heart and with all your soul and with all your mind.' This is the first and greatest commandment. And the second is like it: 'Love your neighbor as yourself.' All the Law and the Prophets hang on these two commandments'" (22:34–40, NIV).

Why are we commanded to love? Why does everything seem wrapped up in that one thing? Because God wants us to be a living body. And the body of Christ, like other living things, does not become alive through the abilities of the members. It becomes alive through the relationships between the members. Love is the organizing force in the body of Christ. Everything else is built on that foundation.

Love is never the easier way, but it's always the best. Showing understanding and empathy in the most contentious kinds of situations can be every bit as miraculous as the healing of cancer.

Questions for Discussion

1. Is it better to avoid cancer or treat it? What tools to prevent cancer in the body of Christ are found in 1 Corinthians 13?

2. People giving their personal agendas the highest priority cause the body of Christ to become unhealthy. Have you ever seen this happen? What were the results?

3. Are believers ever called on to suffer or sacrifice? Why does the American church place such a low priority on this? How can we change?

4. Have you pursued happiness as your primary goal? How is happiness acquired?

5. Jesus was not concerned about fairness while He followed the will of the Father. What does this say to us today?

6. Ministries and churches established on the personality of a strong leader may be tempted to go down the path of self-aggrandizement and human-centered appeals. Have you ever seen this happen? How could it have been avoided?

CHAPTER

14

THE MOST EXCELLENT WAY

*Now you are the body of Christ, and each one of you is a
part of it. And God has placed in the church first of all apostles,
second prophets, third teachers, then miracles, then gifts of healing,
of helping, of guidance, and of different kinds of tongues. Are all
apostles? Are all prophets? Are all teachers? Do all work miracles?
Do all have gifts of healing? Do all speak in tongues? Do all
interpret? Now eagerly desire the greater gifts. And yet
I will show you the most excellent way.*

—1 Corinthians 12:27–31

While no church is perfect, I can't help thinking that smaller, more rural, and less affluent churches offer a distinct advantage over the megachurches that have become so popular—namely, their more authentic relationships. I don't want to spark any great debates; I know of megachurch leaders who emphasize that their "lifeblood" is found in small groups rather than at huge weekend worship services. Still, it's my experience that in smaller congregations, the people naturally tend to be closer. Members tend to depend on one another more and help one another out more often. Their closeness doesn't arise from a formula for church growth. They don't take action out of compulsion or being "shamed" into it. I've seen strong bonds of relationship grow out of the needs of everyday life. Although not always as exciting, these Christ-like relationships seem to be found less frequently in places that are more entertainment-oriented, more organized, more affluent, larger, and more sophisticated.

Despite this advantage, I have seen that numerous church leaders and members seem focused on the goal of growth for the sake of growth. Many want their church to be larger, more affluent, and more sophisticated. However, along the way to building the size of our organization, we may lose sight of what matters. The essence of the body of Christ comes from our bonds of love. Instead of appreciating the value of the small and intimate, we reason that bigger must mean better. I've been involved with large churches and appreciate the resources they can bring to education, fellowship, and funding mission work. Still, size isn't everything.

Lydia and I discovered this recently after we decided to spend more time at our home in the Ozarks region of Arkansas. Although we still own a home in Dallas, we found ourselves wanting to spend more time at a lake house with which the Lord blessed us. I geared down my medical practice to do this and have more time to travel, including watching our daughter play in the 2015–16 basketball season at Oral Roberts University.

PICTURESQUE SETTING

Our lake home is nestled in a picturesque area amid hills, with considerable trees and wildlife. Located "in the boonies," it is miles away from a city of any size. One of the first things we set out to do after settling in was finding a good place to worship. The first weekend, we drove to the church closest to our home, which is a small country congregation about five miles down the road. From the first time we walked in the door, we felt at home. Partially due to the members' isolation from the conveniences available in large, urban areas, they are more dependent on one another.

The church is out of the norm in several ways. For example, it has never sought—nor does the congregation want—tax-exempt status with the Internal Revenue Service. Members want to remain as free as possible from the bureaucratic demands associated with maintaining such an exemption. Nor is the pastor paid as a full-time cleric, so the distinction between clergy and laity is intentionally blurred.

In addition to Sunday services, prayer meetings, Bible studies, and evangelism classes, members frequently get together for food and fellowship, survival classes, and other activities. During the controversies that flared in 2016 about police shootings, the people organized an outreach to show support for the local police and sheriff's departments. Working in cooperation with several other churches, they helped sponsor a "Family of God" gathering with food and fellowship. As you might imagine, dinner on the grounds is a regular occurrence. Individuals freely share vegetables from their gardens and eggs from their chickens at these potlucks. They gather as often as possible for fellowship. They fish and hunt together. They laugh together and cry together. Family maintains a high priority; it isn't lip service but exists with practical actions. The pace of life is slow, too, as if the people are waiting on God to provide opportunities for community.

Testimonies, prayer requests, and swapping life stories are a big part of each get-together. The church members emphasize evangelism, but they do it in the context of developing loving relationships over time, not based on formulas or special events. They don't put on a show; they are authentic and depend on one another. When one member had problems with a water well (no city water in this area), other members brought them buckets of water—without being asked and without a special water-shuttling program in place. They were just living out their lives, trying to help one another as much as possible.

When a family member passes away, the church body organizes to help with food and other assistance. Members don't do this out of a sense of coercion or guilt or to be seen as good people. They just inherently know it's the right thing to do, so they do it to honor God.

A MEMORABLE EXPERIENCE

Our second visit to this church proved to be a memorable experience. One of the members, a man named Teddy, had recently been diagnosed with terminal cancer. Telling him there weren't any effective treatments available, doctors had estimated he had only a few more weeks to live. Although church members had been fervently praying for Teddy's healing, he felt it was time for him to meet the Lord and allowed no anxiety about his situation. His stance reflected his spiritual growth over the years, which had eventually led to members electing him as a church deacon.

On this particular Sunday morning, the pastor brought him to the platform to say goodbye to the members of the church. A crowd of about seventy people—many of them Teddy's family members and friends— had packed into the small sanctuary. The pastor and Teddy chatted for an hour as Teddy recalled events from his earlier years, how he had come to know Jesus as his Savior, and how he had discovered the church. He expressed his appreciation for all the help and friendship he and his wife, Sarah, had received from all the members. Many of the audience members also spoke from their pews to express their appreciation for Teddy.

While I didn't even know these people yet, a tear came to my eye. The session offered an intimate look into the lives of the individuals around me. They obviously touched Teddy, too. He seemed to look at things with more than a glance. As he paused often to take it all in, his eyes shone with light. Teddy constantly smiled and laughed easily; he appeared to be the most content person I had ever seen. He obviously saw this present life in a rich way that most of us cannot fathom. Indeed, he saw things in the context of an eternity in heaven that would begin shortly. He obviously didn't want to leave his friends and family behind. After all, he loved them and would miss them greatly. But he had great joy in knowing what would lie ahead for him. Besides, he drew assurance from the fact that they would join him there relatively soon.

While Teddy returned for another Sunday or two, he was confined at home for his final days. As a result, I didn't have the privilege of getting to know him as well as many others had done. Still, hearing this interview and his sincere gratitude for relationships with other members of the body made a lasting impression. It reminded me of the Christian love Paul described in 1 Corinthians 13. This is what makes the body of Christ alive. It is the Christ-like love that bonds us together in unity. Without it, we are dead.

HEARTFELT AFFECTION

I have witnessed this kind of Christ-like affection through a number of people in this church, such as Bill and Ann, who decided to check out Arkansas after Bill retired a decade ago. They had never visited the state, and on their journey from Florida in their small camper, they prayed for God to show them the perfect place.

"Lo and behold, we ended up in this area," Ann recalls. "We bought an old mobile home, not knowing if we'd stay here or not. It also came with a lot across the street. As we sat on the porch one day, we decided we liked it here and that we wanted to build across the street. Our next-door neighbors said they'd help us build it with their son. That made five of us.

"The day we were ready to put on the roof, a bunch of neighborhood men that we didn't even know showed up via the grapevine. Another neighbor, who had just moved here, came over every day to help—and wouldn't take any pay. Neighbors are always helping their neighbors in one way or another."

Sally calls people in the area her "family." The church and others have helped her and her husband, Joseph, with moving, fixing broken-down vehicles, and even feeding them "just because." Lately, they have been living rent-free in a beautiful home on the lake thanks to a couple from the church who wanted to help them out in their time of need. The owners didn't even know Sally and Joseph. They just knew the couple needed a place to live.

"What a blessing!" says Sally. "The other day, we had an issue with one of our vehicles on the way to town. A lady nearby let us wait inside her shop and watch TV for over an hour while we waited. One of the members of the church saw our vehicle on his way to town and helped my father and Joseph make the repairs. We are truly one big family down here."

Then there is the experience of Ned and Diane. Several years ago, Ned had his left knee replaced. In 2013, doctors diagnosed an infection in the same knee. That forced him to undergo surgery to remove the previously implanted knee joint and to go for eight weeks without a joint in his knee. He was finally released from the hospital after three weeks. It was necessary for him to be administered intravenous antibiotics three times a day for the next six weeks.

Unfortunately, the day after his release from the hospital, his wife had to make a trip to Kansas City. Diane worried about having no one there to care for him. Then the blessings of God started flowing. Before she had to depart, two neighbors had volunteered to sit with Ned. A home health-care agency made arrangements to come and administer the antibiotics. Others promised to bring food for Ned's meals while she was away.

"After that, we felt continually blessed by our church family," Diane admits. "They would provide meals and periodically show up to relieve me so I could go to the store or just take some time off. We will never forget—or feel that we could ever repay—our community for what they did for us during our time of need."

Don't get me wrong. This isn't Mayberry (and the place where Andy Griffith served as sheriff was a fictional place, anyway). As with every town on earth, all-too-human problems and interpersonal conflicts arise and must be resolved. Still, to me it seems that such examples illustrate how the body of Christ can flourish in a setting where relationships and community are emphasized. Such churches are an example of a healthy, breathing, working organism, created by God and given the breath of His life to be His hands and feet in the world. These churches may look different according to the state, region, or country where they exist; there is no perfect formula for structuring a local church. Since we are all different individuals, when we assemble in groups for fellowship, the groups will also be unique. Yet when love is present, the mutual caring, support, and affection will enrich life in a way no earthly fortune, fame, or achievement can satisfy.

AIMING AT THE TRUTH

It has always been my belief that faith and science, or faith and reason, are not incompatible with one another. In fact, they are extensions of the same thing: truth. When I see a healthy church relating to its members like cells of a single body, serving as the hands and feet of Christ in their communities, and taking their instructions from His word, it fills me with the same awe that seeing the marvel of the human body does in my professional practice. The fingerprint of God is on both beings, and knowing the science of how both work just strengthens my faith.

It is a joy to witness the marvels of God's creation, but when I observe the body of Christ and my relations to it in my own life, along with the joy I have also felt a sense of sadness. I have not always acted as a healthy member of the living body of Christ. At times, I have fallen far short in my relationships with others. I wince at the memory of things I have said and done in the past. Though I didn't have evil intent when I said or did them, my human understanding is at times too shallow. I feel many of my efforts for God and for the churches I have attended over the years have been hindered because of this shortcoming. As "Lament," the poem from the introductory chapter, describes, they are wood, hay, and stubble.

Too often, I've tried to do things alone; it seems I haven't been able to trust others. I've tried to be successful as an individual rather than as a member of a body. I have thrown away things that matter and held on to things that don't.

I think most of this has been due to unawareness—ignorance about the importance of relationships. I did not appreciate my role as a member of a living body. There is no way to go back in time and redo what has been done. We have only the present. That is why I am so thankful that forgiveness is available to me. I pray I will be able to forgive others who have failed just as I have.

I will keep trying day by day to cultivate the relationships the Lord is giving me. I think this, as well as being sensitive to the leadings of the Holy Spirit, is the best plan. No matter our shortcomings, the Lord is quite willing to help us move forward from here with His plan for the body of Christ.

As I have come to appreciate the distinction between the organized church and the body of Christ, I have become more aware of the absolute importance of my relationships to other believers and our collective submission to the will of God. I hope this book has helped my readers to do the same. The organized church is an invention of man; the eternal, holy Church is a living organism created by God. The fact that the organized church is an organization does not diminish its value or suggest that it is unnecessary. In fact, it is vital for the effective ministry of the body. Yet we need more. Our walk with God should be a vibrant, authentic, functioning characteristic of daily life—not just something we perform on Saturday or Sunday before we go on with the rest of our week.

It is my prayer that local churches will gain a much deeper appreciation for the vital role they play in the living, breathing expression of the body of Christ in their community. That all members will understand, whether they like it or not, that anyone who bears the name of Christian is on display and under scrutiny from nonbelievers who want to see whether he or she is for real or is just playing religious games. I pray that local churches will fulfill their destiny by applying the principles of life outlined in the Bible rather than just mimicking the ways of the world.

In the last verse before the famous love chapter of 1 Corinthians 13, Paul wrote these words: "Now eagerly desire the greater gifts. And yet I will show you the most excellent way." That most excellent way is the way of love.

Questions for Discussion

1. What advantages do you see in being part of a small church? Of a large church?
2. What did you think as you read the story of church members gathering to express their appreciation for Teddy? What would you think if someone did that for you?
3. Have you ever lived in a community where neighbors came over to help install a roof without asking to be paid? How did that make you look at life?
4. Do you feel you've fallen short when it comes to appreciating the value of relationships? What can you do about it?

A PRAYER

I thank You, Lord, for taking many diverse believers and creating the Church as one living body, with Christ as the Head.

Thank You for creating spiritual gifts and giving them to members. Lord, help me understand that my gifts were not earned and are intended not for my own edification but for building up Your body. Help me to always use my gifts out of a heart of service to others. Help me not to become a hollow shell of a man, using my gifts to appeal to superficial people, with nothing of eternal significance inside me.

Thank You for giving me a mind to think clearly and understand Your words. Thank You for giving me faith to accomplish things seemingly impossible. But help me to never use understanding or faith to promote myself. I pray I will always use these with the well-being of others in mind.

Help our discernment, Lord. Help us to know what is true and not be distracted by the untrue.

Lord, thank You for giving me much in this life to share with others. Thank You for giving me the ability to accomplish much for Your kingdom. But I know this is nothing in and of itself. I pray You will take it all away if I become self-centered and lack Christian charity. Help me to recognize the needs of others in the body and meet those needs, as I am able.

Teach me patience and kindness, whatever the cost. Help me not to desire what does not belong to me. Teach me to be content and to do Your will, as You provide me the strength. Help me not to be proud and boastful, as if I'm capable of doing anything on my own. Help me to honor others, too, especially my elders. Remove ungodly anger from my heart so that I never attack other believers. Help me to shrug off the slights of others and not even remember they occurred.

Forgive me for becoming amused by the evil deeds of others. Help me not to pursue mindless entertainment. Help me avoid the ways of the world and not become entangled in them. Help me not to confuse material gain with godliness. Sorrow brought about from the lies of Satan is all around me in the world. Your Truth brings me joy.

Thank You for giving me the heart of a shepherd. Give me courage and strength to protect those in my charge. Help me to rely on Your strength as I protect them and provide for them. Never let hope fail in my heart but allow me to persevere in Your ways, even when it seems impossible.

Thank You for Your eternal love. Even when the time comes that prophecies, tongues, and knowledge are no more, Your love will remain eternal—unifying the members in Your will and Your words.

Sometimes I feel I know much, but when Your presence surrounds me, I realize that my knowledge is feeble. Thank You for teaching me so I may minister to others.

I pray for Your body in this world, that it would mature and develop into what You desire. I pray we will be bound together by Your love so the world can know You. Give us unity, and help us to know how to preserve it. When unity comes, we will be able to comprehend fully Your eternal love.

Help me to grow as a member of Your body. Help me not to remain a child. I want to mature into the fullness of Your vision.

What seems real in this world is illusory. Through each day, I have only thin comprehension of Your designs. Help me to more clearly see Your will. Help me not to be afraid of becoming open and vulnerable to others in the body. I want to become more fully known by my fellow members.

Lord, I pray You will give me faith to do Your will and hope for the future. But most of all, I pray for Your love to be at the center of all I say and do.

Help me to become a mature member of the body of Christ.

In Jesus's name, amen.

BIBLIOGRAPHY

Benestad, J. Brian. *The Christian Vision: Man and Morality*. Hillsdale, MI: Hillsdale College Press, 1986.

Bonhoeffer, Dietrich. *Sanctorum Communio: A Theological Study of the Sociology of the Church*. Vol. 1 of *Dietrich Bonhoeffer Works*. Minneapolis, MN: Fortress Press, 1998.

Brand, Paul, and Philip Yancey. *In His Image*. Grand Rapids, MI: Zondervan, 1984.

Campbell, R. K. *The Church of the Living God*. Beamsville, ON: Believer Bookshelf, 1985.

Clippinger, John Henry, III, ed. *The Biology of Business: Decoding the Natural Laws of Enterprise*. San Francisco: Jossey-Bass, 1999.

Colson, Charles. *The Body: Being Light in Darkness*. Nashville, TN: Thomas Nelson Publishers, 1992.

Dulles, Avery. *Models of the Church*. New York: Doubleday, 1984.

Eldredge, John. *Waking the Dead*. Nashville, TN: Thomas Nelson Publishers, 2003.

Finke, Roger, and Rodney Stark. *The Churching of America 1776–1990: Winners and Losers in Our Religious Economy*. New Brunswick, NJ: Rutgers University Press, 1992.

Franks, Tommy. *American Soldier*. New York: HarperCollins, 2004.

Gregersen, Niels Henrik, ed. *From Complexity to Life: On the Emergence of Life and Meaning*. Oxford, England: Oxford University Press, 2002.

Guinness, Os. *Dining with the Devil: The Megachurch Movement Flirts with Modernity*. Grand Rapids, MI: Baker Books, 1993.

Gleick, James. *Chaos: Making a New Science*. New York: Viking Adult, 1987.

Holland, John H. *Emergence: From Chaos to Order*. Boston: Addison-Wesley, 1998.

Jenson, Robert W., and Carl E. Braaten, eds. *Marks of the Body of Christ*. Grand Rapids, MI: Eerdmans, 1999.

Johnson, Steven. *Emergence: The Connected Lives of Ants, Brains, Cities, and Software*. New York: Scribner's, 2001.

Jung, Carl. *Man and His Symbols*. New York: Dell Publishing, 1964.

Kelly, Kevin. *Out of Control: The New Biology of Machines, Social Systems, and the Economic World*. New York: Perseus Books, 1994.

Kelsey, Morton T. *Healing and Christianity: A Classic Study*. Norwich, England: SCM-Canterbury Press, 1973.

Lee, Witness. *The Building Up of the Body of Christ*. Anaheim, CA: Living Stream Ministry, 1988.

———. *Further Light Concerning the Building Up of the Body of Christ*. Anaheim, CA: Living Stream Ministry, 1988.

———. *The Scriptural Way to Meet and to Serve for the Building Up of the Body of Christ*. Anaheim, CA: Living Stream Ministry, 1988.

———. *Speaking Christ for the Building Up of the Body of Christ*. Anaheim, CA: Living Stream Ministry, 1988.

———. *The Organic Building Up of the Church as the Body of Christ to be the Organism of the Processed and Dispensing Triune God*. Anaheim, CA: Living Stream Ministry, 1989.

———. *The Perfecting of the Saints and the Building Up of the Body of Christ*. Anaheim, CA: Living Stream Ministry, 1989.

———. *A Thorough View of the Body of Christ*. Anaheim, CA: Living Stream Ministry, 1990.

———. *The Intrinsic View of the Body of Christ*. Anaheim, CA: Living Stream Ministry, 1991.

———. *The Constitution and the Building Up of the Body of Christ*. Anaheim, CA: Living Stream Ministry, 1992.

———. *The Church as the Body of Christ*. Anaheim, CA: Living Stream Ministry, 2004.

Lewis, C. S. *Mere Christianity*. Rev. and enl. ed. San Francisco: HarperOne, 2015.

MacArthur, John, Jr. *The Body Dynamic: Finding Where You Fit in Today's Church*. Colorado Springs, CO: Chariot-Victor Publishing, 1996.

McCaleb, Gary D. *The Gift of Community: Reflections on the Way We Live and Work Together*. Abilene, TX: Abilene Christian University Press, 2001.

Meyer, Christopher, and Stan Davis. *It's Alive: The Coming Convergence of Information, Biology, and Business*. New York: Crown Business, 2003.

Nee, Watchman. *The Holy Word for Morning Revival*. Vol. 1 of *Topics for New Believers*. Anaheim, CA: Living Stream Ministry, 2002.

Ogden, Greg. *Unfinished Business: Returning the Ministry to the People of God*. Rev. ed. Grand Rapids, MI: Zondervan, 2010.

Olson, David T. *The American Church in Crisis: Groundbreaking Research Based on a National Database of over 200,000 Churches*. Grand Rapids, MI: Zondervan, 2008.

Pullman, Bernard, ed. *The Emergence of Complexity in Mathematics, Physics, Chemistry, and Biology*. Princeton, NJ: Princeton University Press, 1997.

Robinson, John A. T. *The Body: A Study in Pauline Theology*. Norwich, UK: Hymns Ancient and Modern, 2012.

Schaeffer, Francis A. *The Mark of the Christian*. Downers Grove, IL: InterVarsity Press Books, 1970.

Schrodinger, Erwin. *What Is Life? With Mind and Matter and Autobiographical Sketches*. Reprint. Cambridge: Cambridge University Press, 2012.

Schweizer, Eduard. *The Church as the Body of Christ*. Richmond, VA: John Knox Press, 1964.

Stedman, Ray. *Body Life: The Book That Inspired a Return to the Church's Real Meaning and Mission*. Rev. and expanded ed. Grand Rapids, MI: Discovery House Publishers, 1995.

Stowell, Joseph M. *From the Front Lines: Perspectives from the Trenches of Life*. Grand Rapids, MI: Discovery House Publishers, 2007.

Wilson, Scott, and John Bates. *Clear the Stage: Making Room for God*. Springfield, MO: Influence Resources, 2015.

Yancey, Philip, and Dr. Paul Brand. *Fearfully and Wonderfully Made*. Grand Rapids, MI: Zondervan, 1980.

NOTES

Introduction: Love Is the Key

1. Eduard Schweizer, *The Church as the Body of Christ* (Richmond, VA: John Knox Press, 1964), 63.

2. "Porn Use in Church Continues to Escalate," *Charisma News*, September 1, 2016, http://www.charismanews.com/sponsored-content/59612-porn-use-in-church.

3. Evangeline Paterson, "Lament," from *Deep Is the Rock* (Elms Court: Arthur H. Stockwell Limited, 1966), in *A Christian View of the Church*, vol. 4, *The Complete Works of Francis A. Schaeffer: A Christian Worldview* (Wheaton, IL: Crossway, 1982), 205.

Chapter 1: Spiritual Reality

1. Carl G. Jung, *Man and His Symbols* (New York: Dell Publishing 1964), 4.

Chapter 2: The Vision

1. Charles Colson with Ellen Santilli Vaughn, *The Body: Being Light in Darkness* (Nashville, TN: Thomas Nelson Publishers, 1992), 63.

2. Stoyan Zimov, "Too Many Christians Don't Love the Church," *Christian Post,* December 10, 2015, http://www.christianpost.com/news/rick-warren-too-many-christians-don't- love-the-church-152196.

Chapter 3: Bodies

1. Schweizer, *The Church as the Body of Christ*, 21.

Chapter 4: Are We a Body or a Business?

1. Greg Ogden, *Unfinished Business: Returning the Ministry to the People of God*, rev. ed. (Grand Rapids, MI: Zondervan, 2010), 41.

2. Ibid., 213–214.

3. J. Brian Benestad, *The Christian Vision: Man and Morality* (Hillsdale, MI: Hillsdale College Press, 1986), 40.

4. Ibid., 41.

5. Paul Saffo, preface to *The Biology of Business: Decoding the Natural Laws of Enterprise*, by John Henry Clippinger III, ed. (San Francisco: Jossey-Bass, 1999), xvii.

6. Ogden, *Unfinished Business*, 41.

Chapter 5: Knit Together

1. Charles Spurgeon, "Unity in Christ," message delivered January 7, 1866, at the Metropolitan Tabernacle, Newington, London, in *The Complete Works of C. H. Spurgeon: Volume 12, Sermons 668 to 727* (Harrington, DE: Delmarva Publications, 2013), 7.

2. Andrea Palpant Dilley, "The Surprising Discovery about Those Colonialist, Proselytizing Missionaries," *Christianity Today*, January/February 2014, http://www.christianitytoday.com/ct/2014/january-february/world-missionaries-made.html.

3. Ibid.

4. Teen Challenge International, "Teen Challenge's Proven Answer to the Drug Problem," review of "The Teen Challenge Drug Treatment Program in Comparative Perspective," by Aaron T. Bickenese, http://www.teenchallengeusa.com/wp-content/uploads/2014/05/1999_NW_review.pdf.

5. Wilder Research, *Minnesota Teen Challenge Follow-Up Study: Results Summary* (January 2011), http://www.teenchallengeusa.com/wp-content/uploads/2014/05/2011_MN_summary.pdf.

6. Minnesota Department of Corrections, *An Outcome Evaluation of the InnerChange Freedom Initiative* (February 2012), https://demoss.egnyte.com/dl/UbSlFaja0t.

Chapter 6: The Essence of Life

1. Steven Ertelt, "57,762,169 Abortions in America Since Roe vs. Wade in 1973," LifeNews.com, January 21, 2015, http://www.lifenews.com/2015/01/21/57762169-abortions-in-america-since-roe-vs-wade-in-1973.

Chapter 7: Natural Power Plants

1. T. S. Eliot, *The Complete Poems and Plays, 1909–1963* (New York: Harcourt Brace, 1963), 153.

2. Colson with Vaughn, *The Body: Being Light in Darkness*, 48.

Chapter 8: Cells: The Members of the Body

1. Steven Johnson, *Emergence: The Connected Lives of Ants, Brains, Cities, and Software* (New York: Scribner's, 2001), 86.

Chapter 9: Unity amid Diversity

1. Ogden, *Unfinished Business*, 33–34.

Chapter 10: Order in the Body

1. Tommy Franks, *American Soldier* (New York: Harper Collins, 2004), 164–65.

2. Len Wilson, "5 Things Geese Can Teach us About Teamwork," from *Lead Like Butler*, by Kent Millard and Judith Cebula (Nashville, TN: Abingdon Press, 2012), http://lenwilson.us/5-thing-geese-can-teach-us-about-teamwork.

3. "Capitalism and Globalization Examined," DiscoverTheNetworks. org, http://www.discoverthenetworks.org/viewSubCategory. asp?id=288.

Chapter 11: Immune Disorders

1. Joseph M. Stowell, *From the Front Lines: Perspectives from the Trenches of Life* (Grand Rapids, MI: Discovery House Publishers, 2007), 28.

2. Michael Gruntman and Ariel Novoplansky, "Physiologically Mediated Self/Non-Self Discrimination in Roots," *Proceedings of the National Academy of Sciences*, March 16, 2004, http://www.bgu. ac.il/desert_ecology/Novoplansky/novoplansky4.pdf.

3. Francis Schaeffer, "The Mark of the Christian," in *A Christian View of the Church*, vol. 4, *The Complete Works of Francis A. Schaeffer: A Christian Worldview* (Wheaton, IL: Crossway, 1982), 20.

4. Stowell, *From the Front Lines*, 28.

Chapter 12: The Dangers of Infection

1. Os Guinness, *Dining with the Devil* (Grand Rapids, MI: Baker Books, 1993), 21.

2. Sydney Lupkin, "Ebola in America: Timeline of the Deadly Virus," ABC News, November 17, 2014, http://abcnews.go.com/Health/ ebola-america-timeline/story?id=26159719.

3. Ken Walker, "Faces of the Persecuted Church," *Charisma*, September 2016, 26.

4. "'Islam Is Peace' Says President," transcript of remarks by President George W. Bush at the Islamic Center of Washington, DC, September 17, 2001, https://georgewbush-whitehouse.archives. gov/news/releases/2001/09/20010917-11.html.

5. Andrew C. McCarthy, "Tashfeen Malik's Jihadist Social-Media Posts Were Deliberately Ignored by the Feds," *National Review*, December 15, 2015, http://www.nationalreview.com/article/428540/tashfeen-maliks-social-media-ignored-dhs.

6. Andrew Husband, "Syed Farook's Neighbors Didn't Report 'Suspicious Activity' for Fear of Profiling," *Mediaite*, December 3, 2015, http://www.mediaite.com/tv/syed-farooks-neighbors-didnt-report-suspicious-activity-for-fear-of-profiling.

7. Katie Pavlich, "Neighbor Didn't Report Suspicious Activity of San Bernardino Killers for Fear of Being Called Racist," *Townhall*, December 3, 2015, http://townhall.com/tipsheet/katie-pavlich/2015/12/03/neighbor-didnt-report-suspicious-activity-of-san-bernardino-killers-for-fear-of-being-called-racist-n2088543.

Chapter 13: The Parasite Known as Cancer

1. Philip Yancey and Paul Brand, *Fearfully and Wonderfully Made* (Grand Rapids, MI: Zondervan, 1980), 20.

ABOUT THE AUTHOR

Ron Bryce, MD, is an emergency room physician in Dallas. He earned his medical degree in 1986 from Oral Roberts University's medical school. A former member of the ORU Alumni Association board, in 2016 ORU honored him as Alumnus of the Year. He is a member of the Christian Medical and Dental Associations and served as CMDA's Texas representative from 2011 to 2015.

A longtime Christian, Dr. Bryce has been a Sunday school teacher, church elder, and church musician and during medical school played piano for a Southern gospel group. He has been a board member for GeoBound missions and for Abundant Life Missions, an organization started by his parents and which focuses its efforts in Haiti. His community involvement has included serving as mayor of Red Oak, Texas, from 2006 to 2007. He was appointed by Governor Rick Perry to the Texas Medical Board and served from 2006 to 2012.

Bryce is married to Lydia Bryce. They have four children: Daniel, twenty-six; Blair, twenty-four; Joseph, twenty-two; and Brooke, twenty.